HEART OF GRAY

Richard

To a Soldier, Patriot and classmate of "Iggy's". Liberty and freedom are won with Sacrifice.

Richard W. Ennus
12.16.2014

HEART OF GRAY

Lt. Raymond "Iggy" Enners, Courage and Sacrifice of a West Point Graduate in Vietnam

RICHARD W. ENNERS

Acclaim Press
MORLEY, MISSOURI

Acclaim Press
— Your Next Great Book —

P.O. Box 238
Morley, MO 63767
(573) 472-9800
www.acclaimpress.com

Book Design: Devon Burroughs
Cover Design: M. Frene Melton

Cover Photo: U.S. Military Academy cadets prepare for pass and review before
a football game in West Point, NY, 1 November 2008. DoD photo by Navy Petty
Officer 1st Class Chad J. McNeeley.

ISBN: 978-1-942613-37-4 / 1-942613-37-7
Library of Congress Control Number: 2016902862

First Printing 2016
Printed in the United States of America
10 9 8 7 6 5 4 3 2 1

This publication was produced using available information.
The publisher regrets it cannot assume responsibility for errors or omissions.

Contents

For my parents Raymond and Gloria Enners, my
brother Ray, and sister Sandra.

For my wife Judy, sons Sean and Ryan, their wives Darby and Lisa,
and grandchildren William, Eliana, Reese, and Evie.

For the Soldiers of Alpha Company, 1-20th
Infantry Regiment, 11th Infantry Brigade, Americal Division who fought
bravely and honorably in the Republic of South Vietnam.

"Upon receiving the LT. Raymond Enners Award
I was truly humbled to be associated with such a decorated soldier and athlete.
LT. Enners excelled because he made those around him better
on the lacrosse field and off.
As my role model, this is the code by which I hope to live my life
as a player and a person."

Kieran Mullins

Winner of the Suffolk County
LT. Raymond Enners Award, 2014

FOREWORD

★ ★ ★

Ray Enners was born and raised with the heart of a true champion and a natural leader. He was revered and loved by those who watched him mature through his formative high school years on Long Island, New York, just a stone's throw south of the United States Military Academy at West Point, New York. This account of Ray's life documents the transformation of his champion's heart to a "Heart of Gray"—a heart, spirit and soul dedicated to the ideals of West Point; Duty, Honor, Country; a heart committed to selfless service; a heart committed to leading America's young men and women during times of future crises for our nation.

Why Gray?

Most everything at West Point is a commanding gray–the mountains, the buildings, the sky in the winter, and most of the cadet uniforms. Where is the inspiration in the color of gray? Well, early in our nation's history, the summer of 1814, a very small American Army wearing gray uniforms decisively defeated the British in Canada. As a badge of honor and in memory of that battlefield victory, the Secretary of War approved the use of Gray for the cadet uniforms. Ray Enners bought into that tradition and joined the Long Gray Line of cadets and academy graduates, heart and soul!

Heart of Gray is a loving brother's life story of 1Lt Raymond J. Enners, a recognized leader at an early age and destined to be a great American leader. Ray's life was cut short when he was tragically killed in a North Vietnamese Army (NVA) ambush at the age of twenty-two. He was fatally wounded attacking a superior force after unselfishly risking his life to save a wounded member of his platoon. For his actions that day, he was awarded the Distinguished Service Cross for extraordinary bravery in combat, second only to the Congressional Medal of Honor.

As you read *Heart of Gray*, you will learn the details of Ray's early life and the process that developed him as a leader. That development process began with his family and his youth on Long Island, New York. You'll learn the values they instilled in Ray as he developed into a star high school athlete and class leader. You will learn how he grew interested in becoming a Cadet at the United States Military Academy at West Point and the factors that convinced him to commit to the ideals of West Point, embodied in its motto "Duty, Honor, Country." You'll understand why there is a Raymond J. Enners Award for college lacrosse, the equivalent of the Heisman Trophy for the best player in college football. You will follow Ray through his four years at West Point and you will learn many of the details of the incredibly demanding academic, physical, moral and leadership development programs. You will follow him through his early days in the Army and the grueling Ranger training at Fort Benning, Georgia. You will live with him in the jungles and rice paddies of Vietnam. You will share the shock and grief of his family upon notification of his death. You will read emotional accounts of his West Point 1967 classmates who knew him best. They knew him as a standout leader among leaders–a beloved member of the class with the prophetic motto, "None Will Surpass the '67 Class!" You will also tearfully read the tributes of so many of his mentors and soldiers after his death.

Americans are living in a dangerous world of complex conflicts–a world that seems more threatening with each passing day. The threats have been and will continue to be some combination of economic, religious, cultural, environmental, and military. If America is to prosper, your children, grandchildren, loved ones and friends will be committed to the long campaign and will pay the price. You will want them to be led by the likes of Ray Enners.

I'm so honored to be Ray's classmate,

John S. Caldwell, Jr.
Lieutenant General, USA (Retired)
USMA Class of 1967

AUTHOR'S NOTE
★ ★ ★

The events that took place on the battlefields in South Vietnam as presented here reflect official sources and documents and the best recollections of those individuals in Ray's command and those with whom he fought. Sometimes the "fog of war" can blur details and the sequence of events. On a limited number of occasions, I added commentary to the battlefield events based on my understanding of how the events unfolded from others merely to tie the sequence of incidents together. I relied on Ray's classmates for their poignant anecdotes of their days at West Point, Ranger Training and experiences during their military careers. I documented their recollections in extensive interviews. Dad and Mom's collection of photographs, news articles, memorabilia, and memories of Ray before and after he was killed were instrumental in providing factual data as was my sister Sandra's memory of Ray growing up. In some cases, I relied on my memory of my experience at West Point and in the U.S. Army.

Facts from declassified official documents added realism to the accounts of what transpired July through September 1968. Historical accounts and opinions of the war in Vietnam came from books written by well-respected authors. These accounts in no way represent the official position of the United States Military Academy at West Point, the U.S Army, or U.S. Government.

Where it applies to those who fought for America in wars of the past or are currently serving, I capitalize the words "Soldier" and "Veteran." Freed Lowrey, Ray's classmate, proudly brought this to my attention during our interview. It is out of respect for these individuals that I do this and am honored to do so.

Throughout the book, I highlight Ray's leadership style. An important part of leadership is character, and that primarily develops during childhood and adolescence. Parents, relatives, coaches, and others help to define a person's character during this socialization process. Those values are unique to the individual. What is not unique are the many principles of leadership documented in books and manuscripts over the course of many centuries. Ray was not born with all of the qualities an effective leader should possess. He learned and practiced principles of leadership that he thought would best influence others in a positive way.

It is with great pleasure that I donate fifty percent of my net proceeds from this book to the United States Military Academy at West Point. In honor of combat Veterans who served in all branches of the military, fifty percent of my net proceeds will be donated to CAUSE (Comfort for America's Uniformed Services), a Veterans support organization whose programs help wounded warriors begin the normalization process and re-entry to home and community.

MAPS
★ ★ ★

PROLOGUE
★ ★ ★

The pointman suddenly stopped. He whispered to Sergeant Matheson that he heard something three meters inside the tree line. Matheson gave the hand signal for "halt" and peered inward toward the dense bamboo laden thicket. 3rd platoon dropped to one knee with weapons at the ready.

It was 18 September 1968 in the midst of Phase III of the *Tet* Offensive. Operation Champaign Grove was no ordinary mission, no ordinary combat assault. It was a brigade size maneuver in the western jungles of Quảng Ngãi Province designed to provide relief to an under sieged Special Forces Camp at Hà Thanh and block the North Vietnamese Army supply routes to Quảng Ngãi City.

Tired, irritable, and worn from the challenges and intensity of combat duty, Alpha Company was conducting a combat sweep southwest of Hà Thanh, and Ray's platoon was in the lead. They came across a large rice paddy with a hedgerow to the north. Sergeant Matheson was walking "slackman" as 3rd platoon crossed at the narrow point in the paddies and maneuvered around a finger of thick shrubs and trees. Heading west, they hugged the thicket at the edge of the paddy field for about seventy-five meters.

No more than ten seconds after Matheson took a step into the thicket, an element of the communist North Vietnamese Army (NVA) opened up with bursts of AK-47 fire. The pointman dove behind a paddy dike. Matheson's M16 flew out of his hands. He fell where he was hit. Blood gushed from the open wound. The tree line exploded with enemy RPD machine gun and automatic weapons fire. From the first drop off Ray's platoon, in a riveting display of firepower, responded with M16 and M79 intensity, blasting the tree line. The NVA were dug in—well concealed in the thick underbrush.

Matheson sought the scant cover of a nearby dike so the NVA could not see him. He pressed his arm against his side to curb the bleeding from the six inch gash in his right elbow where the bullet exited. As one of Ray's squads pushed into the thicket trying to lay down suppressive fire, the intense enemy onslaught repelled their advance.

Under a hail of bullets from 100 meters back, Ray crawled forward through the paddy field. He reached Matheson's squad and Squad Leader Sergeant William's position. Ray tried twice to reach the wounded squad leader, but the NVA fire was relentless.

While First Lieutenant McNown, Platoon Leader of 2nd platoon, advanced one squad through the finger of trees to outflank the enemy, his Platoon Sergeant, Sergeant First Class Wright, maneuvered two squads and two M60 machine gun crews around the outcropping, placing them in position to support Ray's attempt to rescue Matheson. Ray repositioned his three squads.

What transpired next was truly an act of passion and courage, an act of sacrifice and selflessness, which characterized Ray's moral fiber.

A little more than thirty hours prior to the firefight in the early hours of the morning, elements of the 3rd North Vietnamese Army Division ambushed six of Ray's men as they were returning from their listening post and ambush site and engaged his platoon's perimeter near Câo Nguyên, one and a half kilometers north of the Special Forces Camp. Ray's platoon suffered several casualties, and that weighed heavily on him.

There is never an easy day in combat. Operations are rarely perfect, and not every Soldier survives the peril of a combat mission. Ray trained for this. He received one of the best undergraduate educations available. West Point saw to that. And, the fifty-seven day grueling experience at Ranger School gave him the technical and tactical competence to lead a platoon in combat and the psychological strength to face any challenge. No training, however, teaches a leader how to handle the loss of a Soldier in their command. He would deal with it. He would save his mourning for a quiet evening at base camp. He had to—the mission was all-important, and he had other Soldiers to look after. Despite the hardships of combat, Ray loved leading. That is where he felt comfortable.

On the battlefield, a leader must carefully balance accomplishing the mission with looking after his men. A complex thought process, it transcends normalcy of thought, particularly in the heat of battle. Ray balanced both. He possessed the warrior ethos that inspired confidence and resilience in his team. The humane side of his personality demonstrated empathy and kindness. He took his military obligation seriously; saw his service as a call to duty. The honor of fighting for American values, he thought, was for a cause greater then himself.

Heart of Gray is a chronicle about my brother First Lieutenant Raymond J. Enners and his will to "choose the harder right instead of the easier wrong." It's an account of selfless acts of courage and provides an insight into how he lived his life and how the values he lived by influenced his actions. He was a Soldier who embraced not only the mission, but his Brothers in Arms and American ideals.

This is a story of emotion and intensity. It's a story of leadership and sacrifice. It's a story about a young leader, a member of the Long Gray Line, who, with honor and pride, embraced West Point's values of Duty, Honor, Country and lived his life with no illusions, with no expectations of gratitude.

HEART OF GRAY

Lt. Raymond "Iggy" Enners,
Courage and Sacrifice of a
West Point Graduate in Vietnam

Part I

★ ★ ★

LEADING IS A CHOICE

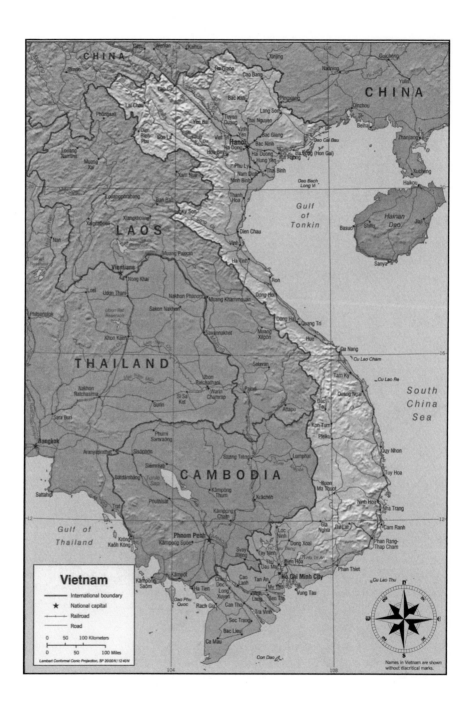

Vietnam

International boundary
★ National capital
Railroad
Road

0   50   100 Kilometers
0   50   100 Miles

Lambert Conformal Conic Projection, SP 20°00'N/12°40'N

Names in Vietnam are shown without diacritical marks.

Chapter One

REALIZATION

"Everyone needs to realize that they set an example for someone.
It is so very important to be the best example you can be.
The lives of young people can be changed forever
by seeing people do what is right."

Stanley Tyron
WW II Prisoner of War

It was 8 July 1968. Anxious and with little knowledge of what would transpire, Ray departed for the Republic of South Vietnam. Mom and my sister Sandra drove Ray to JFK Airport in Jamaica, New York.

Unfortunately, I could not see my brother off, as I was a Yearling at West Point and had just begun summer training at Camp Buckner. I did talk to Ray on the phone before he departed and wished him well. The sport of lacrosse, West Point, the U.S. Army, and just being brothers intertwined our lives in many ways both before and after his death. I followed his lead, and that was a challenge, a sequence of hurdles one higher than the previous. He was three years my senior, and I remember my first day of high school. School Director Ms. Annette Brancaccio knowing I was Ray's brother, asked me, "Are you as good as your brother?" A question with many contexts, but its connotation taught me to embrace the fact that in life, every day is a test, and putting forth the effort in all endeavors would surely pay off. I responded, "I hope to be." Ray had a strong influence on me, and my exchange of words with Ms. Brancaccio inspired me to work hard and live up to his standards. Doing so over the years made me a better athlete, husband, father, and leader.

Sandra was in high school and remembered the two days leading up to his journey to Southeast Asia. My parents threw a going away party prior to Ray's departure. His friends from West Point and high school attended as well as relatives. "It was a fun party," said Sandra, "lots of camaraderie among Ray's friends, a keg of beer and cigars; no talk of war or fears of what might lie ahead." Mom and Dad supported Ray's decision to volunteer because it was what he wanted to do. Our patriotic upbringing heavily influenced his and my strong sense of duty. They supported all of us in our decisions as to the path we would take in life. "There was no dissension that I can recall, no outward show of fear or emotion, only support," recalled Sandra.

Dad departed for work on that day. "He never missed a day of work, but perhaps this was easier on him," Sandra recalled. "It was a hot summer day with clear blue skies outside the large glass windows where we waited at the airport gate for Ray's flight to board for the West Coast." Ray was dressed in his starched, crisply pressed khaki uniform. "I was always so proud of him," said Sandra. "We all made small talk, but I could tell there were 'lots of nerves,' and he was anxious for the goodbyes to end and get on his way." They hugged and kissed goodbye. Ray boarded the flight for San Francisco. Mom and Sandra saved their tears for after he departed. Ray would have wanted it that way. Sandra said, "Mom and I didn't say much on the ride home. I think we all had our fears, but they remained unspoken."

On the trip home from JFK Airport Sandra recalled vivid memories of her time with Ray. On occasion, she would tag along with Ray to meet his friends. It was an indication of Ray's kindness and for Sandra a feeling of importance. She recalled Ray teaching her to drive his prized Austin Healy. "Bucking up and down the street, teaching me to shift gears, he wanted me to drive the car while he was away after I passed my driver's test," said Sandra.

Ray arrived in San Francisco at 9 p.m. He hopped on a bus bound for Travis Air Force Base where he would meet up with classmate and lacrosse teammate Ed Sullivan. They would depart at 2 a.m. the next morning on a Trans World Airline (TWA) jet bound for Biên Hòa, Đồng Nai Province, Vietnam. Their flight would stop in Hawaii and Okinawa for refueling.

Ed grew up in Baltimore, Maryland, and retired from the Army as a Lieutenant Colonel. He served as a Platoon Leader with the 2-14th Infantry, 3rd Brigade, 4th Infantry Division in the II Corps Tactical Zone (Central Highlands) of Vietnam. During his tour, he earned the Combat Infantryman's Badge (CIB), a Bronze Star Medal, and four Air Medals. He also served as the S3 (operations) and later as XO (Executive Officer) with the Manchu's, the elite military unit that guarded South Korea's security on the Demilitarized Zone (DMZ).

During their flight, Ed later recalled, "It was an odd feeling flying to Vietnam. Certainly, [it was] like going into the unknown. I learned a lot from training, heard a lot of stories, and read books." The sights, the sounds, the horrors of combat that Ray and Ed were about to encounter, however, could only be truly understood by those who served in that environment. Would all of their schooling and training over the course of the last five years prepare them for the real thing?

It was late morning (local time) 10 July, when the B-727 made its final approach into *Biên Hòa*, thirty-five kilometers northeast of Saigon. The cabin stirred with activity. Ray, Ed, and their fellow Soldiers onboard scurried about to get their belongings together. There had been plenty of time for sleep and reflection on the twenty hour journey from San Francisco, but now the realization of going to war set in.

Within a few hours, Ray and Ed would report to the Relocation Center in *Long Bình* that signified the beginning of their combat tour. For all practical purposes, it was also the beginning of their military career. Combat is a unique experience for all those who serve and for officers, Non-commissioned Officers (NCO's), and enlisted, it paves the way for advancement in the military. Ray volunteered for Vietnam, as did the majority of his West Point classmates. He felt it was his duty. He wanted to do his part—it would measure his worth as an Army Officer.

During the trans-pacific flight to Asia, I do not know what was going through Ray's mind. I doubt that he thought about the political turmoil that existed in Vietnam, the fall of Điện Biên Phủ or the unpopular rule of Ngô Đình Diệm, Prime Minister of South Vietnam. I doubt the visual of the Buddhist monk setting himself on fire commandeered his thoughts. I suspect he thought about family or his past experiences and lessons learned from high school and West Point. Maybe, still, he tuned in to his most recent experience, Ranger School.

"The trip over wasn't too bad at all, but it was long. It took twenty hours," said Ray in a letter to my parents and Sandra. At the Replacement Center, he spent two days in processing, the typical stuff, signing and ensuring the accuracy of documents. Ray was surprised to find out that the G1 (personnel administration) changed his orders from the 25th Infantry Division to the Americal Division located in the I Corps Tactical Zone just below the demarcation line that separated North Vietnam from South Vietnam. Nonetheless, this was common as officers were assigned to units where they were most needed at the time.

Ray's first impressions of Vietnam, as recorded in a letter to my parents provide insight into the diversity and nature of war. "It's amazing how it can be safe in one area and five minutes away there can be a firefight going on. You can hear artillery and mortars firing constantly, and choppers and jets flying around the clock. It all looked so peaceful when we were in the air flying in, but you know it's not."

Amidst the sounds of war, echoing in the distance, Ray and Ed found a place to sleep. When they awoke, it was time for dinner. Fortunately, there was a Navy club close by. They walked down a dirt road, concertina wire on both sides, and came to a bunkered structure. As they went inside, they were surprised that the club was air-conditioned and had a beautiful stone faced bar. Two Army lieutenants wearing the coveted black and gold Ranger Tab seeking food and a beer in a Navy club, in a combat zone—H*mm*...? They sat down and had a steak dinner. Ed remembered it vividly, "It was wonderful."

"It was pitch-black when we left," recalled Ed. "There wasn't a light anywhere." It was a little unnerving walking down the dirt road to their sleeping quarters after a couple of beers. They didn't have weapons, helmets, or flack vests. They had no protection at all. "We didn't know if someone was going to 'jump' us," said Ed, "or worse yet, be ambushed."

What a challenge it was getting flights to their final destination. At the relocation center, a Major on his second tour casually implied that if they came back at 0400 hours the next morning, he would try to get them out to their units. Ah, the agony of disorganization. Ed said, "You were basically on your own."

Early the next morning Ed flew on to Pleiku. Ray boarded a C130 for Chu Lai (on the coast) to begin a seven day indoctrination training program.

"You sit in the dark on the tarmac until you finally get on a C130 with red lights inside, and you're off. It was eerie," said Ed. He arrived safely in Pleiku at dawn, only to find sappers had just attacked the city. In a nonchalant and routine manner, the locals were policing up the dead bodies.

Welcome to Vietnam!

Ray's indoctrination program in Chu Lai lasted four days, not the seven previously told. The war in Vietnam was a war of insurgency fought using small unit tactics. Platoon leaders were among the most vulnerable (to enemy fire), and as a result, the turnover rate was high. In between his indoctrination training, he was able to swim in the South China Sea a couple of times, which was refreshing and almost like being at Gilgo Beach on Long Island.

It was 17 July. Ray hopped on a UH-1 Iroquois helicopter, commonly known as a "Huey", in route to Đức Phổ, Quảng Ngãi Province, the 11th Brigade Headquarters and firebase called Landing Zone (LZ) Bronco. Located on the coast, adjacent to Highway 1 and Mount Montezuma, LZ Bronco served as headquarters to several Marine and Army units to include the 101st Airborne Division. There, Ray joined his unit, Alpha Company, 1st Battalion, 20th Infantry Regiment.

Upon arrival in Đức Phổ, Ray was advised that his unit was in the field on a "Search and Clear" operation southwest of the city. He was eager to take on his responsibilities as platoon leader of 3rd platoon, about thirty-five Soldiers. The Table of Organization & Equipment (TOE) for a light infantry platoon was forty-two men; however, it was common to be under strength due to turnover and the needs of personnel elsewhere. The suffix for his call sign would be "three-six."

Ray's commanding officer was Captain William Adams, call sign "six." Adams had been in the army for about ten years. He received his commission through Officers Candidate School (OCS) and arrived in Vietnam as a First Lieutenant. In the field for ten months and operating as a Reconnaissance Platoon Leader near the Laotian border, he was a highly skilled officer. "Captain Adams was a fine officer," recalled John McNown. "He had a lot of experience in how to handle troops." Adams knew the tactics of routing out insurgents, having spent several months in the Special Forces. Promoted to Captain in April 1968, he replaced Captain Sario Caravalho on 5 May, then Commanding Officer of Alpha Company.

Ray was certainly equipped mentally and tactically, to take on his new responsibilities, but he had no experience leading a platoon in a hostile, war torn environment. So, what does it take? His classmates and subordinates shed some light on this. Interestingly enough, their comments and examples are not partisan to the military. Modern day concepts of leadership originated from the military many centuries ago, and parallels can be drawn for those leading organizations in the public or private sector.

Classmate Harry Rothmann said,

> If you are a new leader in a combat unit, no matter if you are a lieutenant, captain, or a major, and you say I'm in charge and I'm responsible for this unit, and you'll do what I tell you to do, you'll fail in a heartbeat. The most valuable thing to me was to listen to the squad leaders and platoon sergeants. You must be in tune with

those who you are leading, get to know them as quickly as possible, and know their strengths and weaknesses. And then employ their strengths.

Harry hailed from Valhalla, New York. He served in Vietnam as a Platoon Leader in Alpha Company and as Company Commander of Delta Company in the 3-506th, 101st Airborne Division. For his service, he earned the Combat Infantryman's Badge (CIB), two Bronze Star Medals for meritorious service, and an Air Medal. He also served as a Company Commander of 2-39th, 9th Infantry Division in Fort Lewis, Washington, and at the Pentagon Army War Plans Division. He retired from the U.S. Army as a Colonel.

Knowing Ray, after meeting members of his platoon, his first job was to develop a level of trust not only within his platoon members but also laterally across Alpha Company and with his superiors. He had the confidence in himself to seek advice and ideas from his superiors and subordinates alike. He showed that in prior leadership roles. Doing so, particularly with his subordinates, would establish a basis of trust in the unit–trust being the foundation of building a cohesive team. Trust is also how you influence subordinates to follow. "If you can build that trust between you and your people, then everything else will fall in line," said Harry. "If you don't, the capabilities and benefits of an M60 machine gun or an M79 grenade launcher don't mean a thing."

Ray was good about keeping us (on the home front) abreast of his activities. On 19 July he indicated, "There has been very little contact in the past month; however, this is probably the lull before the storm." The 11th Brigade was expecting a large-scale offensive in the next month or two. He went on to say, "The NVA and Charlie, [as the American Soldiers called the Việt Cộng], have moved back into the mountains to regroup, train, and resupply. We're expecting a mortar attack here at Đức Phổ sometime in the next few days." The "intel" that Ray received and wrote about was clearly the NVA's forthcoming plans to launch the third phase of *Tet*.

The missions for Alpha Company and 3rd platoon for the month of July were Search and Clear type operations originating from LZ Bronco, located on a hill top about four kilometers west of the coast just east of Đức Phổ. At 150 meters (492 feet) high, it was a field base and launch point for combat assaults, Search and Clear missions, and refitting after a mission. Search and Clear missions inserted platoon or company size (some times larger) elements into hostile areas to locate enemy units or individual insurgents and engage to kill or capture.

For the first twenty-three days of July, Alpha Company was in the field on missions and returned to LZ Bronco only twice. Extended missions moving from one grid location to another covering tens of kilometers each day was the nature of warfare in the I Corps area. Punji stakes soaked in urine and excrement, booby traps, anti-personal mines, and very little sleep caused injury and some fatalities as they humped through the "bush." Enemy snipers heavily camouflaged in "spider holes" picked off Soldiers on patrol. Living in tension was the norm. Being alert just wasn't enough to survive. It took teamwork, tactical competence, extensive communications, and sheer grit. Hot and humid weather caused fatigue and heat exhaustion. In addition, the constant rain during the monsoons was just pure aggravation.

During the late summer and early fall, the 1-20th operated primarily in Quảng Ngãi Province which was an unusually hostile area, a hotbed of Việt Cộng activity particularly near its southern border with Bình Đinh Province. Prior to U.S. involvement, the Việt Minh, a communist-influenced nationalist group, sympathetic to the North, was particularly adverse to French colonial rule. As a result, they raised havoc in Quảng Ngãi City as well as the rural areas. They integrated themselves into the local population to the point where it was a significant challenge to determine friend or foe. They joined forces with the Việt Cộng guerrillas or National Liberation Front, against the U.S. and South Vietnamese Army in all four tactical zones supported entirely by the North. Ambushes, sniper fire, and sabotage were common; booby traps prevalent–anything to disrupt the South Vietnamese Government from progressing with their western philosophies of governing.

While Ray was conducting Search and Clear operations in the jungles of Vietnam, I was at Camp Buckner patrolling day and night, firing most of the hand-held weapons in the U.S. Army's arsenal, and learning the subtle techniques of day and night navigation. I could identify with what Ray was experiencing to some extent, except the overly harsh conditions and *real* bullets whizzing overhead.

Aside from the perils of combat, Vietnam was geographically a hostile environment. The jungle was indifferent to those who braved its habitat. Young or old, it did not matter; all were susceptible to its horrendous discomforts and irritations. In its peculiar way, the jungle swallowed up all that was human, all that was sane, and all that was logical. It made disorder out of order and obscurity out of clarity–or, maybe that's just war.

"We were in water all day long, and your feet would swell and turn to mush," said Squad Leader Sergeant Al Matheson. Some Soldiers were susceptible to "trench foot" or "immersion foot," commonly called, "jungle rot." Soldiers carried ample amounts of foot powder and plenty of dry socks. "You dried your feet off all the time," said Matheson.

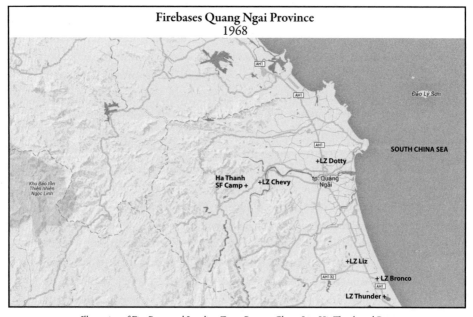

Illustration of Fire Bases and Landing Zones Bronco, Chevy, Liz, Hà Thanh and Dotty

Matheson hailed from Huntington, Long Island, New York. After graduation from high school, he went to the draft office in Brooklyn and volunteered to serve. "I wasn't prepared for college, so I decided to work for a year," said Matheson. "I realized I wasn't going anywhere." He decided to volunteer as he had a low draft number. His first assignment was Fort Carson, Colorado. During his tour in the Rocky Mountain state, he attended and graduated from the NCO Academy at Fort Benning, Georgia. He earned the Combat Infantryman's Badge in Vietnam along with two Purple Hearts, one for shrapnel received on a night ambush in February 1968. The second award received during the battle of Xã Ky Mao on 18 September. During that battle southwest of the Hà Thanh Special Forces Camp, Matheson would be connected to Ray in a very unexpected, yet everlasting, way.

"Leeches, there were so many leeches," said Matheson. They were common in the mountains and valley streams but more of an aggravation in the mountains. Hanging and dropping from trees, leeches one to one and a quarter inches long, attached themselves to a Soldier's neck, boots, and fatigues, often times undiscovered, as focus on the mission was first priority. "Even blousing your fatigues and then double tying them around your boots with an extra lace did not prevent them from getting to your feet and legs," said Matheson. Soldiers sprayed them with mosquito repellant and burned them off to rid themselves of the blood-bloated pest. "Those little guys would suck you dry," he said.

Just another day in the jungle, another discomfort in the Boonies.

"As soon as we would cross a river, we would have a 'leech check.' That was a great time for the NVA to attack, but they never did," said Specialist Fourth Class Ray DeVincent, Radio Telephone Operator (RTO) for Captain Adams.

Ray DeVincent was born in Woodside, Long Island, New York, and raised in Farmingdale. "It was a good thing I was drafted; it was bad in the late sixties with so [many] drugs," said DeVincent. "Some of my friends were on drugs, and I didn't want that."

DeVincent had a wry sense of humor. As Adam's RTO, DeVincent was responsible for maintaining communications with the battalion Tactical Operation Center (TOC) and securing company and battalion codes and radio frequencies. "I was an important person; everyone protected me," said DeVincent. "In fact, one time we were being mortared, and I pulled him [Captain Adams] on top of me. Adams said, 'What the hell are you doing?' I said, 'Protecting your codes.'"

Commanders carefully selected their RTO's; they had to be strong in the face of enemy fire. It was a dangerous job. They were always no more than four feet away from the commanding officer in a firefight, and the three-foot antenna clearly signaled, to the enemy, *here I am, shoot me first*. If the commanding officer was hit, the RTO would take over communications, requesting "Medivacs" (medical evacuations) or artillery fire.

Matheson and DeVincent met at Schofield Barracks, Hawaii, in 1967. They trained with the 11th Brigade, Americal Division—created 1 July 1966 and bound for Vietnam. They lived in the "Old Quads" seventeen miles north of Pearl Harbor, and trained in the Kahuku Forest Reserve located at the northern end of the rugged Koolau Mountain Range in preparation for their combat assignment. It was horrific training, simulating the dense vegetation of the mountains and jungles of Vietnam.

Late at night in early December they boarded the *USS Gordon*, a steam turbine Naval troop carrying vessel that accommodated over 390 officers and 4,800 enlisted personnel, plus the crew. Heavily armed with four single five inch guns, four twin 40 mm guns, and twenty 20 mm guns, they set sail from Honolulu Harbor for Qui Nhon Harbor, South Vietnam, with the balance of the 11th Brigade. During the seven day trip, they mingled with other Soldiers and formed friendships, some that exist today.

In the valleys and hilly areas at the base of mountains, Soldiers grappled with elephant grass often times six foot in height. They called it "razor grass." "It [would] seriously cut you," said DeVincent. "It was also suffocating; you [couldn't] breathe in it. It [stole] your oxygen. There was one time, I was ready to turn myself over to the other side," he said laughing. "It [was] horrible."

Such was the life of a combat Soldier in the jungles of Vietnam.

They were hardly sunshine patriots. When a mission called, they went under any circumstances, any hour of the day or night, rain or shine. At least ten times during combat sweeps in late July, elements of Alpha Company engaged the NVA and VC due to sniper fire or ambushes.

Immediately after joining his unit on the 17th, Ray was leading his platoon on a sweep. What would he run into—a sniper, an enemy squad, or would it be a large unit? In an enemy saturated territory, a combat leader cannot assume anything. "[On the 22nd], we were searching and clearing a village and were hit by a sniper. One of my men was wounded, and we didn't even see the sniper; he was so well hidden." While the medic attended to his wounded Soldier, Ray's RTO immediately requested a Medevac.

Medevacs—consisting of two pilots, a medic, and crew chief- had incredibly dangerous jobs. Flying UH-1 Huey helicopters with a red cross plainly visible on its doors, they flew in horrible weather, at night, in and out of "hot" landing zones taking enemy fire as they flared in, on the ground as they loaded the wounded, and on departure. Their call sign was "dustoff." Their discipline and courage saved many lives. In most cases, wounded Soldiers would be in a hospital within an average of thirty-five minutes.

Specialist Fifth Class David "Doc" Bushey was Senior Medic for Alpha Company during the time Ray served in Vietnam. He grew up in North Baltimore, Ohio, a small town of 3,400 residents. He was about to enter the University of Findlay when he received a draft notice. Classified as 1A, Bushey was given a choice by the Army: attend either Officer's Candidate School or medical school at Fort Sam Houston, Texas, and become a medic. He chose medical school and enrolled in the thirty-six week course. For his service in Vietnam, Doc received the Combat Medical Badge (CMB), Bronze Star Medal, and Purple Heart; the Purple Heart, a result of shrapnel wounds received 17 May in the Battle of Nui Hoac Ridge.

Combat Medics are rare individuals, receive extensive training, and operate under the most chaotic situations on the battlefield. In the midst of a harrowing firefight, they maneuver to the wounded, stabilize the Soldier, and ensure a safe extraction. "Combat was quite a shock," said Doc. "You had to push things out of your mind because the next day would be the same all over again." Doc recalled one incident with a Soldier whose appendix was about to burst, and due to the terrain, the Medevac was not able to set down on top of a mountain.

Smitty, one of Captain Adam's RTO, had a strobe light. The Medevac asked them to mark their exact location. It was pitch black dark. "Smitty stands up, extends his arm, and turns the strobe light on," said Doc. Snipers homed in on the bright light and began firing. The Medevac pilot said, "I'm going to drop a 'jungle penetrator.'" Smitty looks at [Doc] and says, "What's a penetrator?" When Doc arrived in Vietnam, "jungle penetrators" were not in use but became more prevalent during his time in the field. They dropped the "jungle penetrator," and Smitty grabbed it. He twisted and turned it, trying to figure out the subtleties of its design. "He finally pulled a lever down and four little, oh they were like feet, came down. It was like a seat harness." Smitty and Doc positioned the Soldier in the seat, secured the safety belt, and the Medevac pulled him up. "We're taking fire, and Smitty is standing up there with this strobe light. That's the kind of stuff that happens," said Doc.

In addition to the Dustoff, Ray requested a scout dog from battalion headquarters to search for the insurgent. With the assistance of the scout dog, 3rd platoon located spent cartridges where Charlie was lying. This was Ray's first brush with the reality and the perilous face of combat.

Combat units frequently used dogs. Sentry dogs guarded base camps. Scout dogs detected and found the location of ambush sites, mines, booby traps, and caches of weapons or food. On a patrol the scout dog would smell each Soldier and be alerted to a different smell in the bush. Tracker dogs hunted the enemy down. It was not terribly difficult in the jungle as the smell of the VC and NVA were noticeably different from the GI. "We could smell the enemy," said Sergeant Matheson, "what they ate even in the jungle."

"Two nights later we were hit at night while we were in our [company] perimeter," said Ray. "They had a few automatic weapons and grenade launchers. We didn't have any casualties. Right now we are securing LZ Thunder, and I don't know for how long." That was 23 July after finding and destroying a VC tunnel south of LZ Bronco.

For the next six days Ray's platoon provided security for the Battalion Tactical Operations Center at LZ Thunder. Heavily equipped with ammunition, canteens topped-off with water, equipment taped and tied down on their harnesses to avoid rattling noises, and faces painted in the usual camouflaged pattern, the patrols went out each day and night to search for the enemy. They intentionally avoided heavily traveled trails, as the odds of ambushes were higher. The winding tangle of a muddy trail made it even more dangerous. As Ray would soon find out, that, too, was an imperfect tactic. The enemy knew the terrain. They hid where they could achieve a tactical advantage. On five occasions Ray's platoon encountered VC insurgents, three near Pho Trung resulting in one Killed in Action (KIA); one west of LZ Thunder resulting in one Wounded in Action (WIA) and one Captured in Action (CIA); another half kilometer from LZ Thunder resulting in one KIA; and yet another one kilometer from LZ Thunder resulting in one KIA. His platoon captured eleven VC suspects near the same location and evacuated them to LZ Bronco for interrogation.

On two occasions in July, Alpha Company conducted combat assaults based on suspected VC sightings. One was on 27 July in the Sơn Hà District, ten kilometers east of the Battalion TOC. Ray's platoon completed their airlift to An Mỹ Trại at 0925 hours. Well camouflaged, two VC engaged elements of his platoon with sniper fire. Ray maneuvered his squads towards the snipers, and the firefight that ensued resulted in one VC KIA. One escaped. Sniper fire hit a helicopter from the 174th Aviation Battalion four times, one time in the main rotor blade, fortunately without injuries.

At 1110 hours, Alpha Company found a VC tunnel complex near their insertion point booby trapped with a Chi Com (Chinese Communist) grenade. Carefully disarming it without incident, they continued to search the area. They came across another tunnel at 1515 hours harboring a VC suspect. He would not come out, and after repeated attempts to coax the suspect from the tunnel, the insurgent was shot and killed. At 1540 hours, 3rd platoon was extracted.

At 1605 hours while in route to LZ Thunder, Ray's platoon received heavy ground fire less than two "Klicks" (kilometers) east of their initial engagement. Helicopter gunships accompanying the extraction also took heavy fire. Returning fire, the gunships killed six Việt Cộng guerrillas.

By now, Ray had been incountry for a couple of weeks, and I could detect a great amount of concern in Mom's voice when we talked on the phone. It was during my Yearling summer at West Point. On 27 July 1968 just prior to leaving on a weeklong Recondo exercise at Camp Buckner, I wrote my family a letter, and in my parting paragraph I said, "Don't worry about Ray, Mom. I think about what he's doing, but I don't worry. He is a good soldier. When I write to him, I don't mention it [the war]. He can take care of himself." Both Dad and Mom carried the burden of a son at war as so many parents did.

I tried in so many ways to allay her fears. Each of us dealt with them in different ways. Mom went to work at Prestige Labels. Dad had his work. Sandra kept busy at school with studies and athletics, and I, of course, had my hands full with summer military training. None of us ever lost sight of Ray's combat assignment, his purpose. We were very proud of him.

On the last day of July, Alpha Company received orders for a combat assault, destination - the western slope of the mountains twenty kilometers west of Qui Nhon City, Bình Định Province. Anticipating a firefight, anxiety levels were high. First pickup was at 0613 hours in the morning and the last lift completed at 0647 hours. The landing zone was cold, no insurgent contact. At 0926 hours, Alpha Company found Hồ Chí Minh sandals, VC uniforms, and one M-72 LAW (Light Anti-tank Weapon). They destroyed the LAW in place. At 0940 hours, they moved through the thick wooded area just south of Tho Loc and uncovered a cache of weapons: AK-47's, .30-caliber ammunition, NVA clothing, and blasting caps. Captain Adams airlifted the contents of the cache to LZ Thunder.

Alpha Company continued their sweep. In the early afternoon less than one kilometer west of the cache, they engaged two insurgents clad in black pajamas, killed one and captured the other. At 1616 hours the insurgent POW led Alpha to a well camouflaged two foot by six foot "L" shaped tunnel. Searched and secured, the tunnel was empty of weapons and food. A Huey airlifted the POW to LZ Bronco for interrogation.

As the light of day faded to gray, Alpha Company established their Night Defensive Position (NDP) west of Highway 1 and northwest of Phước Thành.

Dinner consisted of C-Rations, less than a culinary delight, but to a hungry Soldier it sufficed. There were twelve different menus, not that you could usually choose. A C-Rat typically consisted of one canned meat (better cooked with trioxane heating tablets than eaten cold), one canned fruit, bread or dessert, and an accessory packet containing coffee, salt, pepper, and an assortment of other items. Oh, yes, and toilet paper, a must when relieving yourself in the bush. Hold on to your P-38 can opener; there were only twelve per case of C-Rations. Bartering was popular: I'll give you my ham and lima beans if I can have your pound cake or fruit cocktail. Under that scenario, you were a fool to barter away either your pound cake or fruit.

Ray established ambush sites with rotating shifts outside his platoon sector with lanes established for those "manning" the site to return to the perimeter. He learned early on that establishing front and rear security, assembly points, "code-words," communications, and "kill zones" where a trail curved maximized the effect of an ambush and minimized danger to his men. With "claymores" set, M16s pointed down the trail, and the M60 "pegged" on the kill zone, they settled in for the night. The Soldiers lay quiet and still, like a panther eying its prey. That evening and early the next morning, quiet befell 3rd platoon; only the *poo-kay, poo-kay, poo-kay* of the Tokay Geckos surrounding the NDP could be heard. There was no insurgent contact.

Fortunately, there were no fatalities under his command in July. Unfortunately, that would change as the third phase of *Tet* heated up, and larger scale combat engagements with the NVA became more prevalent.

America's involvement in Vietnam began in 1961, but for Ray, it had only just begun. His initial experience in close combat was certainly eye opening, and he was learning every day. Combat tested his mental and tactical abilities. It also tested his character and leadership capabilities under highly stressful conditions. Ray was proud of his unit. He loved his team and found inspiration in each team member, just as he did as captain of his high school football and lacrosse teams.

Some individuals are more comfortable following. Leading is a choice, as it was for Ray, an internal fiery desire to influence others in a course of action that was in the best interest of the organization and each team member. The roots of which began at an early age in a small town in New York.

Chapter Two

MR. MACHINE

"Leadership is not a talent or a gift. It's a choice.
It's not complex, but it's very hard."

General Stanley McChrystal
USMA 1976

It was the spring of 1962, Ray's junior year of high school. I remember watching one of his lacrosse games toward the end of the season. A defenseman cleared the ball to Ray, who was standing near the front of the opponent's goal. Ray had a clear shot, an easy score. Instead, he signaled to Josh Butts, his teammate, to sprint toward the goal, where Ray passed it off. Josh shot and scored. It was Josh's fiftieth goal, a personal milestone and record for the season. "No guts, no glory," they say. Ray certainly had the guts but was not interested in the glory. The team was all-important. That's the way he was.

Ray's character and desire to lead had its origin in Farmingdale, Long Island. It's where we grew up. With a population of a little more than 4,000 people at the time, it was small town America with a relaxed, comfortable feel. Most of Farmingdale was in Nassau County, but our home on 83 Beechwood Street was in Suffolk. The county line cut our street in half, and as a result, we attended schools in Melville and Dix Hills.

We were middle class Americans. We had what we needed, maybe not always what we wanted. Living in a 1,700 square foot house, I shared a second floor bedroom with Ray while Sandra occupied the room across the hall.

Dad was a member of the New York City Photo Engravers union. He was an artisan with a pair of talented hands and a keen mind, who used machine tool routers to etch printing plates, what has become a lost art. I remember him telling us that, as a photo engraver, he etched the printing plates for the Johnny

Walker Scotch print advertisement. He worked the second shift, so we did not see him much during the week, but on the weekends, he was there for us, and with little sleep, always attended our athletic contests on Saturday.

My parents raised us to be patriotic Americans right to the core. As a child, I remember attending the Memorial Day parade on Main Street in Farmingdale. It was quite a sight, bands blaring and flags waiving. On appropriate occasions Dad would place the American flag in its holder attached to the front of the house. He served in the Army Air Force (AAF) during World War II, and that had an influence on Ray *and me* as to how our futures evolved. Dad joined the service on 29 September 1942, served honorably, and completed his service 10 April 1946, well after the Armistice. As an instructor at Chanute Field, Illinois, he taught classes of 5-30 men in heat treatment of aluminum and steel. As a Staff Sergeant with the 37th Air Depot Group in North Africa, he was shop supervisor and led a twelve man team conducting sheet metal repair on battle damaged P-51 Mustang fighters and B-17 Flying Fortress bombers.

He was a very wise man and approached every challenge in a logical, systematic manner; was firm, but not overbearing. First Lieutenant Alfred S. Foy, Division Supervisor, wrote on 1 April 1944 in a letter of recommendation, "Sergeant Enners is known to the undersigned officer as a man whose character, ability, adaptability, and leadership is excellent. He is very energetic and has the respect of those who serve under him."

My parents were married sixteen months prior to my dad deploying for his eleven month tour in North Africa and they lived in a small apartment in Bethpage. Mom became pregnant with Ray just prior to my dad departing for his overseas tour and as a result decided to move in with her parents. She worked in a bank, and the money she earned went straight into savings, as did my father's service pay. They were saving to buy a piece of property for a home; they relished the American dream.

Ray was born in Rockville Centre, New York, 5 November 1945, five months prior to my father returning home. Mom remembers picking my dad up at the Mineola train station after his tour of duty. "It was a glorious day, so good to have him home," she said. They purchased the property at 83 Beechwood Street, Dad began building the home that Ray, Sandra, and I lived in during our childhood and adolescent years.

Mom raised the three of us and provided all of the support any kid could ask for. She was caring, thoughtful, and wanted the best for us. Shuffling us to and from baseball practices and games was a common task, as well as dance classes for my sister. Mom attended all of our athletic games, home or away, and my sister's dance recitals. She and Dad were our most enthusiastic supporters, always encouraging us to practice and work hard at any endeavor. Whether it was trumpet lessons for Ray, drums lessons for me, or flute lessons for Sandra, Mom was always on the go and exhausted at the end of the day. She, like most moms today, wanted us to experience all that was available to youngsters at that time.

We were fortunate to have a strong family support system. Our grandparents lived within two to three miles of our home, and Dad's brother lived one street away. I remember Easter and Thanksgiving dinners at my Grandmother Enner's house in Farmingdale. The entire family - grandparents, aunts, uncles, and cousins - gathered for these festive occasions. Today, as I think back, they remind me of Norman Rockwell's painting *Thanksgiving*.

Our parents emphasized those values that their parents' modeled–be respectful and caring of others, be responsible for your actions, always tell the truth, work hard, and demonstrate humility. These values grounded Ray as they did my sister and me. They were a meaningful part of our socialization as kids and adolescents. Humility, in particular, oftentimes comes from the challenges we face in life. It comes from the challenges we seek, the challenges we conquer. All of us sought challenges–it was a way of life. Raised in the Lutheran faith, Sunday school, church, and later confirmation solidified our faith and the foundation of our upbringing.

As a young boy, Ray loved camping and fishing. New Hampshire was a great location to vacation. During the summer for eight years straight, my parents rented a cabin on Lake Winnipesauke near Wolfeboro. Before dawn each morning, Ray was up before breakfast and paddling the rowboat out to his favorite fishing hole. Perch and sunfish were prevalent, not a bountiful meal, though. Occasionally a lake bass would find itself attached to the hook. Now, that was edible. It was a daily competition to see how many he could catch. When he was not fishing, he was water skiing behind my dad's seventeen foot American Finn wood lap-streak motor boat. Powered by a 40hp Evinrude outboard motor, it would barely get you up on one ski. Nonetheless, we had fun; we all learned to ski.

My father and mother encouraged us to get involved in athletics. Mom played basketball for Bethpage High School. Dad ran track and played football at Farmingdale High School; he was fast and played smart. He received a partial scholarship to play football as a tailback at Wake Forest University, when the university was in the town of Wake Forest, North Carolina. Unfortunately, his parents did not have the additional funds to send him to college. He did eventually play for a semi-pro team on Long Island. Ray and I started with baseball. Ray played short-stop; I played third.

Mom and Dad loved sports. Athletics were always a major part of our upbringing. They knew that physical activity was a benefit to overall health. Athletics at Half Hollow Hills (HHH) High School taught us sportsmanship and the importance of winning and losing with dignity. It taught us that competition makes one work harder, and perhaps the greatest lesson of all, how to be a teammate and active team contributor.

One of the highlights of any teenager's growing up is getting a driver's license. At seventeen, I remember Ray receiving his license. He used Dad's car, a two-tone blue and white 1954 Chevy Bel Air with a three speed column shift. At the time, most automobile manufacturers did not use undercoating, and as a result, the floorboards began rusting to the point that we could see the roadway. What a sight! His friends called it the "cancer wagon," a little embarrassing when he went on a date. The standing joke among his friends was if the brakes failed, you could always use your feet to stop the vehicle.

"Ray loved to have fun and could be as mischievous as he was serious," said Sandra. "On the rare occasion he was home to 'babysit' me when I was younger, he would fill the water pistols for both of us and chase me around until we realized we inadvertently wet down the dining room wallpaper. Other times he would place me in the center of the lacrosse goal to act as a goalie in the backyard so he could practice placing his shot."

Beginning in his first year of high school, Ray played football, basketball, and lacrosse. He excelled in football and lacrosse. In his junior year of football, his teammates nicknamed him "Mr. Machine." Ray always gave 100 percent. As captain of both the lacrosse and football teams in his junior and senior years, he worked his teammates hard, believing that nothing in life worthwhile was achieved without effort and hard work. Getting the maximum results out of his team members he knew would surely pay off, not only in terms of winning, but also in any challenge that life presented. Ray learned at an early age, however, that you must first expect it of yourself. He knew intuitively that a person must know himself or herself first and model those behaviors in a way that generates respect. Then and only then can he expect it of others.

Ray derived competence from knowledge, experience, and practice. He knew that teammates not only responded to moral and physical strength but also to expertise. In the same vein, as it relates to the military, he would later find Soldiers responded to a leader's technical and tactical proficiency. He worked himself and his teammates hard to improve his and their level of competence.

As Ray matured during his high school years, his leadership style became evident to all. It manifested itself in his deepest beliefs instilled during childhood and adolescence by our parents, and his teachers, relatives, coaches, and elders. He had a clear understanding of "how his socialization led to his belief system." His values acted as a North Star, a guide for how he would lead. Had he not led with his values, he would have suffered the ridicule of not being authentic, and teammates would have quickly lost respect and trust. Author Jim Collins said it best, "Leadership begins with not what you do but who you are." If Ray's moral values like integrity, respect for others, accountability, and hard work were the fuel for leadership, then his motivation and learned skills are what ignited him to do what was right under a given set of circumstances.

Ray used influence, not authority, to lead his teammates. This, perhaps, is the least understood aspect of leadership. Position in the organization has little to do with leadership. Inspiring, encouraging, and guiding others in a positive way would be his "signature" style at West Point and Ranger School, and in leading his platoon in Vietnam. He felt this method would drive the right behavior. Joe DePinto, USMA 1986, said, "Great leaders achieve results through influence. Their influence is attained through a strong set of values, nobility of character, and by service to others."

Like all good leaders, Ray was a creator of energy, not a drain. He inspired and encouraged others to improve on and off the athletic field. He was competitive, enthusiastic, and optimistic–his demeanor painted that type of picture. He was coachable, always willing to take sound advice to improve his performance. Others trusted Ray, never doubting his sincerity or sense of right. He also set expectations–guidelines that clearly described how the team or organization should function and operate. Ray did both through his body language and through actions, not words alone.

Perhaps, "tough love" works. That is how Bill Martens coached to get the best out of his players. Ray and I played for Martens in both football and lacrosse. We both credited him, in part, with instilling the discipline necessary to live life with a purpose.

Ray was the quarterback and place kicker. In both his junior and senior year at Half Hollow Hills, he made the Suffolk County All-Star football team. Sam Goldaper, columnist for *The Herald Tribune*, in an article said, "Enners, although playing for a weak Half Hollow Hills team, still came up with the rating of the best passer in Suffolk County."

Charles Clark of *Newsday* in his 4 December 1962 article said, "Ray Enners of Half Hollow Hills is a player who can probably take his pick of colleges on the strength of his lacrosse playing alone. Rated the best passer in Suffolk, Enners does everything with class." In the same article Coach Lou Howard, Amityville High School, called him "probably the most under-rated player in Suffolk."

As a place kicker, he also excelled. "What makes Enners so successful in his place kicking?" asked a journalist. "Practice," replied Coach Martens. "He practices all the time. When we're having other drills on the field, he'll get the manager or somebody and go over and help him practice place kicks."

Typically, ends or running backs carried plays to the huddle from the coach on the sidelines. Coach Martens permitted Ray to call his own plays against opponent William Floyd High School, a highlight of his high school football career as a senior. The coach's high level of trust in Ray helped build his confidence as well as skills development. They won the game by a wide margin, 58-12. That year the coaches in Suffolk County selected Ray for the first team, All-Suffolk County team, as quarterback.

For the last 200 years, Lacrosse, originally called "stickball," was always and still is the "fastest sport on two feet." It originated with the eastern Canadian First Nations people in the early 1600's and spread south into America among the Huron and Iroquois and then spread to the Native Americans of the Plains by the Algonquians in 1832. Stickball was most popular in the Great Lakes, Mid-Atlantic, and Southeast regions. It is truly America's oldest sport.

On the curved end of the stick, elders intricately wove netting to hold the ball. Typically constructed of spruce trees roots, the netting eventually gave way to deer gut. Deer hair comprised the inside of the sinew stitched deerskin covered ball. The goals were sometimes several miles apart with no side boundaries.

Steeped in tradition and the heritage of the Native American culture, the origins of the game taught young boys, too young for battle, to become warriors. Rituals before and after the event contributed to the honor, respect, and mystic nature of the game. Weyand and Roberts in *The Lacrosse Story commented*, "In its primitive form, the game was extremely rough so as to accustom young men to close combat." [*The Lacrosse Story* by Alexander M. Weyand and Milton R. Roberts (Baltimore: Garamond/ Pridemark Press), p. 54.] It required hand-eye coordination, agility, speed, and endurance. The game epitomizes the ultimate team sport.

The stick or "La Crosse," as it later came to be known, was a symbol of reverence, skill, and bravery. Elders, who played as young boys, typically handed their stick to future generations, with philosophical carvings on its shaft. A wise Cherokee elder once carved a proverb on his grandson's stick. "You must first master yourself, before you can lead others." Ray embraced the true meaning of this ancient proverb in athletics and later at West Point and in the military. To him, it meant meet every challenge with ethics, optimism, and a spirit of hard work, and use the lessons to lead others toward an outcome that was beneficial to the organization.

It was in this sport where Ray made his mark in high school athletics. During the early 1960's the game began to gain in popularity. It was and still is the fastest game played on turf, real or otherwise. Little did he know at the time that athletics, particularly lacrosse, would be a contributing factor in his becoming a decorated Army Officer. Similar attributes that were required in lacrosse like mission focus (winning), leadership, skill, teamwork, and physical and psychological stamina were also necessary to be an effective officer in the military, particularly in a combat environment.

Ray played at five foot, nine inches tall and 170 pounds. He wore jersey #26. In 1962, his junior year, under Coach Martens they were undefeated 13-0, and Ray had 35 goals and 39 assists to help the team win the Suffolk County Championship.

In his senior year, he did not score the most goals, but he had the most total points, that is, the sum total of goals and assists. With three games to go in the season, he had scored 23 goals and had 53 assists in nine games for a total of 76 points. In that year he far surpassed the record of 48 assists set two years earlier by Billy Ritch of Huntington High School and helped Half Hollow Hills win the Mohican Division Championship. Billy later played Attack at West Point. Coach Bill Martens said, "Enners is a great competitor, and right now he's in top condition. He loves the game."

As an attackman, he typically played behind the cage (goal), feeding the ball to either attackmen or midfielders cutting in front of the goal with a thirst to score. Even today, much less fifty years ago, it is more prestigious to score goals. That wasn't Ray. He was a playmaker. He did not want the fame or the glory. He knew an assist was just as important as a goal.

In 1963, his senior year, Half Hollow Hill beat their archrival Huntington High School 10-8. Ray received the game ball for his efforts. After more than fifty years that ball now sits on a shelf in my grandson Will's, bedroom as a reminder of his great uncle's competitive spirit as well as Ray's determination and team oriented work ethic.

Mary Anne Pettit, Chris Pettit's wife, recalled Huntington playing Half Hollow Hills in lacrosse in 2014. As she watched her grandson play, she said, "It seemed like yesterday that Ray and Chris played against each other in high school. I can still see it. After the game they shook hands and smiled because they knew they would be playing together at West Point."

Chris Pettit, who became a close friend of Ray's, was an All-Suffolk County football and lacrosse player from Huntington High School. Coach Adams recruited Chris to play lacrosse at the Academy. After graduation from West Point and the arduous training that followed, he became Battery Commander of an air defense missile site in Germany. He also served a tour in Vietnam as a Ranger with an advisory team and earned two Bronze Stars for meritorious service. He joined Lehman Brothers in 1977 and over time rose to become partner and President and Chief Operating Officer.

Suffolk County coaches picked Ray as a first team All-County choice for the position of Attack. He was also the coach's pick for the All-Long Island lacrosse team. The competitive nature and warrior spirit that became a part of Ray in lacrosse also became a part of him as a combat leader.

Ray demonstrated a strong sense of leadership as President of his junior and senior classes and a member of the student counsel. He also graciously accepted the Long Island Athlete Scholar Award in his senior year.

West Point was on Ray's radar screen, in fact, his interest had its origins as early as ten years old. My Aunt Mary and Uncle Jim Walton invited us to the Yale Bowl on 5 November 1955 where Yale hosted nationally ranked Army in what was to become one of Yale's greatest upsets in football history. Prior to the game, about 1,000 Cadets marched on to the field and whistled "On, Brave Old Army Team." My aunt remembered Ray saying, "Aunt Mary, that's where I'm going to school." She said, "You mean Yale?" "No", he said, the other one." Ray was impressed. Before a roaring crowd of 61,000 fans, Yale walked away that day with a 14-12 victory. For many years after, a black and gold Army pennant hung on the wall behind his bed.

In Ray's junior year of high school, Bill Martens contacted Coach Jim "Ace" Adams at West Point. Coach Adams and Assistant Coach John Orlando had an interest, a sincere interest. "Baltimore, Maryland, was the original hub to recruit players," recalled Adams. Long Island, however, was gaining in prominence as Howdy Meyers, football and lacrosse coach at Hofstra University, popularized the sport by convincing high school football coaches to have their players play the game in the off-season to stay in shape.

Coach Adams remembered that John Orlando would also talk to high school coaches; Billy Ritch at Sewanhaka High School and Cliff Murray at Huntington High School were good sources of top talent. As the interest of the coaches at West Point grew, so did Ray's. He thought the Academy was for him.

Dad and Mom thought a family trip to West Point would give Ray a better understanding of the Academy. There, he could witness the environment and visit with the coaches. I remember it well. West Point was alive with activity that Friday in late January, students walking to classes and cadets exercising. We watched the basketball team practice at Gillis Field House.

The massive granite, predominately Gothic Revival architecture of the buildings was intimidating and the views of the Hudson Highlands from Trophy Point spectacular.

During our tour, we stopped at Battle Monument on Trophy Point. Ray was particularly impressed with its inscription. "In memory of the Officers and Men of the Regular Army of the United States who fell in battle during the War of the Rebellion [Civil War] this monument is erected by their surviving comrades." In 1897, as an acknowledgement of respect, courage, and service to the country, retired Secretary of War Lieutenant General John M. Schofield dedicated Battle Monument. At the dedication ceremony he said, "For the true Soldier and officer never forgets what he owes to the men he commands."

A tradition at Trophy Point that began in the late 1800s and continues today is the firing of the cannon for Reveille and Retreat signifying the beginning and the end of the business day. It also provides the opportunity to pay respect to the American flag.

While at Trophy Point, we noticed what looked like segments of a large chain painted black. We later found out that, although President Thomas Jefferson established West Point as a military educational institution in 1802, its role in American history dated back to the Revolutionary War. General George Washington, in his *Sentiments on a Peace Establishment* sent to Alexander Hamilton in 1783, said, "The importance of this last mentioned post, is so great, as justly to have been considered, the key of America." Washington assigned the Polish born engineer Thaddeus Kosciuszko the task of building a well-fortified garrison at West Point in 1778, and Washington transferred his headquarters there in 1779.

Located on the Hudson River, West Point was a strategic garrison along a major British supply route from New York City to Lake Champlain. In 1778, a chain 1,700 feet long that stretched from West Point to Constitution Island prevented British warships and supply vessels from reaching the northern end of the Hudson River. Links of the Great Chain weighing ninety to 120 pounds each were floated on logs across the river and secured to the other side. Impressive, Ray thought. We continued on our tour.

Mom could not help but notice the cadet chapel visible from the Plain. Constructed of native granite and dedicated in 1910, its architecture is a combination of Gothic and Medieval designs. At first glance, the chapel appeared to be constructed into the side of the mountain. The pipe organ is the largest church organ in the world, and the great Sanctuary Window inscribed with the West Point values Duty, Honor, Country impressed us all. Ray's excitement grew.

As we continued our tour, Ray could sense the dedication and discipline as could I; for this was, of course, a military installation, in fact, the oldest continuously occupied military post in America. A blanket of history covered these hallowed grounds.

On our return trip to Farmingdale, we talked about West Point, academics, the military, playing lacrosse, and the fact that West Point was a breeding ground for developing leaders, including Robert E. Lee, Ulysses S. Grant, General Dwight D. Eisenhower, General Douglas MacArthur, and General George S. Patton. Nothing about the Academy came to mind that Ray did not like.

For the next several months, Ray's interest grew primarily based on our visit but also the research he conducted at the local library. He came across a speech given by President John F. Kennedy to the graduating class in 1962. President Kennedy said, "West Point was not built to produce technical experts alone. It was built to produce men committed to the defense of their country, leaders of men who understand the great stakes which are involved, leaders who can be entrusted with the heavy responsibility which modern weapons and the fight for freedom entail, leaders who can inspire in their men the same sense of obligation to duty which you bring to it." Ray liked the ring of that. He embraced that philosophy. He was always willing to help others and inspired them to improve.

Although Ray had a scholarship to play at Rutgers University under Coach Bob Naso, after our trip to West Point and all the research, he decided the Academy was for him.

Admission to the Academy was by either a Presidential appointment or more commonly a senator or member of the House of Representatives, called a congressional appointment. A certain number of qualified alternate appointments were available to athletes recruited in the various intercollegiate sports. The latter was Ray's ticket to West Point.

In a letter dated 26 April 1963 from the Department of the Army, The Adjutant General's office, Ray's dream came true. West Point selected Ray for admission to the Academy. It was at the United States Military Academy Ray would play lacrosse, the sport he loved, hone his leadership skills, and grow as a young man.

Leading an athletic team, a combat unit, or any other type of organization is a test, a daily feat that can be very rewarding. Ray chose to lead at an early age. For him, not doing so was not an option. He enjoyed challenges. He wanted the responsibility, the accountability, not for the glory, but because leading was where he felt comfortable, and that is what he enjoyed.

Yes, he was Type A. Perhaps our parents influenced him. Perhaps his football and lacrosse Coach Bill Martens and subsequently Coach Adams at West Point influenced him. Perhaps still, for Ray, leading was a calling.

Chapter Three

OUT FRONT

For it has been said,
all that a man hath will he give for his life;
and while all contribute to their substance
the soldier puts his life at stake,
and often yields it up in his country's cause.
The highest merit, then, is due to the soldier.

Abraham Lincoln
March 18, 1864

A half-world away and for the first eleven days of August 1968 Alpha Company continued their security mission for LZ Thunder, patrolling and establishing ambush sites day and night outside the perimeter of this firebase. Engagements were sporadic; the Việt Cộng in several attempts tried to infiltrate the base camp perimeter. Subjected to enemy RPG and mortar fire pulling security missions at Firebase Thunder was no less threatening or dangerous than an all-out firefight in the bush.

On 3 August Sergeant Matheson became a member of Ray's platoon taking over responsibilities for 3rd squad. "I was out for a few days with a kidney stone," said Al, "and when I came back, I had the honor of joining Ray's platoon." Matheson knew Ray was a West Point graduate and soon found out Ray attended Half Hollow Hills High School, a major sports rival of Huntington High School where Matheson attended. Ray mentioned that his classmate Chris Pettit also spent his high school years at Huntington High.

Matheson recalled, "I remember writing my parents, telling them that Ray was intense and serious and that we'd put him in his place and lighten him up a bit—teach him the ropes [said jokingly]. Lieutenant Enners was all army, all soldier."

It was 10 August a little after dark. First Lieutenant John McNown flew to LZ Thunder in a helicopter to join Alpha Company. "My first ride in a helicopter," said McNown. A driver from battalion met him at the LZ, and in a matter of minutes they were on their way up a small rise to a bunker reinforced with densely woven sandbags, filled with dirt. He dropped his rucksack and walked into the bunker where he met Sergeant First Class Wright.

As they walked to the command bunker, Wright said, "Captain Adams is away; you'll probably be the platoon leader [for] 2nd platoon." Second platoon was the only platoon without an officer. Wright also said, "Lieutenant Enners is in charge until Captain Adams returns."

McNown grew up in north central Missouri, raised in a military family. His father was a retired Air Force Officer. Two brothers on his mother's side retired from the Air Force, one enlisted and the other an officer. He attended South Missouri State College and received his commission as a 2nd lieutenant through the Reserve Officers Training Corps (ROTC) program. "That's all I wanted to be, an infantry soldier, an officer," said John. At the Battle of Hà Thanh on 22 September, he was awarded the Bronze Star Medal for Valor. He also received a Bronze Star Medal for Meritorious Service, Air Medal, Combat Infantryman Badge and two Purple Hearts, one received at the Battle of Hà Thanh and the other south of LZ Cork on 8 November 1968.

He recalled his first encounter with Ray. "As I arrived, they [the command bunker] had maps out reviewing the operation for the next day," said Mc-Nown. "It was so hot; you cannot believe how hot it was." Mission planning on the firebase typically took place inside fortified bunkers with little to no air circulation. At times, it was oppressive. McNown noticed this particular bunker had a small fan and barely any light. Everyone had his shirt off. Sweat pouring down his face, McNown shook Ray's hand as Ray introduced himself. Ray said, "You will probably have 2nd platoon, but that would be confirmed by Captain Adams."

"Ray was really friendly. He was a good fellow to be around; he had a lot of self-confidence and a good attitude about everything. I remember on the first night when I arrived at the company, he spent twenty minutes with me and told me about himself, how long he'd been there, which wasn't much longer than I'd been there, maybe about three weeks." Ray was the senior lieutenant in the field for Alpha Company and was in charge in the absence of the company commander.

Lieutenant McNown took over 2nd platoon the next day. His call sign suffix would be "two-six." The prefix for call signs changed frequently to confuse the enemy. Three more commonly used, recalled McNown, were "hairy bison," "skillful skater," and "joyful target." McNown never liked "joyful target" as it was a contradiction of terms. Sergeant First Class Wright would be his platoon sergeant.

Ray's indoctrination to his unit was uneventful as was McNown's indoctrination. That is not always the case. Lieutenant Colonel William D. Guinn, Battalion Commander, 1-20th Infantry recalled one unusual incident that involved him and a new platoon leader.

At the time, the North Vietnamese Army began providing combat troops to some of the Việt Cộng units near the coast via a trail that originated in the mountains west of their location. Brigade headquarters pulled the 1-20th back to the coast with the mission of conducting Search and Clear operations against both the NVA and VC.

Lieutenant Newberry arrived at LZ Thunder, the field headquarters at the time for the 1-20th. Having never been in combat, Newberry would join his unit in the field the next day. After Lieutenant Colonel Guinn's helicopter became available, he, Jerry, the Battalion Commander's RTO, the S3 Battalion Operations Officer, and the "newbie" lieutenant lifted off. They were in the air for maybe fifteen minutes, and an outcropping of rocks suddenly appeared through the jungle canopy. Adjacent to the rocky outcropping and a finger of trees they spotted a trail. As they flew over the trail, Lieutenant Colonel Guinn saw an enemy soldier below dressed in green clothing. He said to the crew, "We've got NVA down there." He told the helicopter pilot, *"Circle it! Circle it!"*

The 1-20th recon platoon was the nearest platoon Lieutenant Colonel Guinn had to the outcropping, and it was about a mile away from his position. Guinn called the recon platoon leader on the radio: *"Get here as fast as you can, we have some NVA penned up."* Guinn's helicopter circled the area, and the door gunner fired his M60 machine gun at the outcropping of rocks. They hit a few NVA, but some escaped.

Over the radio, Guinn could hear the pilot. *"I'm low on fuel."*

Impeded by the jungle terrain, the recon platoon was on the way, but slowly. Impatiently, Lieutenant Colonel Guinn said to the pilot, "Land us on that trail," pointing to the trail below. Just as they flared-in to land, Guinn saw an NVA with a Rocket-Propelled Grenade (RPG) under the rock outcropping aiming the RPG at Guinn's helicopter. With an M16 on automatic, he opened fire. The bullets ricocheted off the rocks and hit the insurgent. While still in the air, they threw grenades in an attempt to scatter the NVA into the open. The pilot landed, blocking the NVA's retreat west toward the mountains. The recon platoon arrived just minutes later, but most of the NVA had escaped. "It must have been a large squad or an NVA platoon," said Guinn.

Guinn's chopper returned to base, refueled, and took Lieutenant Newberry to join Captain O'Leary's company. Upon landing, Lieutenant Colonel Guinn introduced Captain O'Leary to his new platoon leader. In a conversation with Guinn later, O'Leary said, "Newberry got down on his knees and threw up." Newberry said, "That son-of-a-bitch [Guinn] is crazy."

That was Newberry's welcome and indoctrination to combat in the jungles of Vietnam.

William D. Guinn retired from the U.S. Army as a Colonel. He graduated from Tennessee Military Institute and received his commission in 1952 as a 2nd Lieutenant from the University of Tennessee ROTC program. Prior to his second tour in Vietnam, he led rifle and weapons platoons, an airborne combat support company, and a Long Range Reconnaissance Patrol (LRRP) Company. He was the Senior Military Advisor and Deputy Province Advisor in Quảng Ngãi Province shortly before becoming battalion commander for 1-20th. During his two combat tours, he received the CIB, two Silver Stars, Legion of Merit, two Bronze Stars, an Air Medal, a Purple Heart, and three Vietnam Crosses of Gallantry.

The NVA, sometimes called the Peoples' Army of Vietnam, were a fierce, well-trained fighting force. They were small in stature, moved quickly and quietly like ghosts in the night, traveled light, and knew the terrain. They could move to within ten meters of a U. S. Soldier without detection. They were resourceful. They strategically hid caches of food and weapons in the jungle as did the VC. They built hospitals and hid in underground tunnels. Fortifications were booby-trapped, another hazard to contend with in the bush.

Lieutenant Colonel Guinn recalled one mission. A rifle company in the battalion found an NVA underground field hospital in the forest. They secured the area and searched the premises. "It had equipment that enabled them to do major thoracic surgery," said Guinn. It also contained a brass "still" for making alcohol to treat the wounded. "As soon as I saw it, I grabbed it, put it on the helicopter, and sent it back to Đức Phổ." He intended to bring it back to the States at the end of his tour, but unfortunately, it was destroyed in a fire prior to his departing.

The high temperatures and humidity were miserable. The damp, musty smell of the jungle brought no memories of home for this was tropical Asia. And the swarms of indiscriminant mosquitos added a significant discomfort to the already unbearable conditions in the field. Heat casualties took their toll. "It was up over 100 degrees Fahrenheit, and the humidity was horrible," said McNown. "You just couldn't carry enough water. At night, the temperature would drop down to about 90 degrees Fahrenheit. I don't think I slept for the first week [I was incountry]. I don't think anybody did. By the end of each day, your uniform turned from green to white from losing so much salt."

"I remember we were always wet," said DeVincent. "Even on dry days, we were wet because we were always sweating. And, if [we weren't] sweating, it was raining."

Because it was so hot in August, Sergeant First Class Wright told Lieutenant McNown to chew tobacco to keep his mouth moist. "I'm 'boppin' along [chewing tobacco], feeling real macho," said McNown. All of a sudden, a sniper opened up. He dove into the rice paddy and swallowed the tobacco. He threw up for the rest of the day. McNown said, "That was the last time I tried chewing."

The next day on the 11th, Alpha Company maneuvered into position to act as a blocking force along the railroad that ran parallel to Highway 1. "There was a berm about six to seven feet above the paddies, and we were behind that," said McNown. "Two of the other companies from battalion were pushing in toward us."

At 1600 hours as Ray's platoon swept the area, the pointman discovered a "hooch." Two VC insurgents tossed grenades from the hooch. Ray's platoon moved into position and engaged the enemy, resulting in two VC killed. The grenade wounded one National Policeman. Inside the hooch, they found an M16 and a .30-caliber carbine. That evening Ray and his platoon set up a NDP while second platoon detained two VC suspects and turned them over to the National Police. Captain Adams flew in that night to rejoin Alpha Company.

Thinking back to that first day in the bush, McNown said, "That first day was a real eye-opener for me. It was my first firefight as soon as we came off the mountain. We had two or three more encounters with the VC in the next week." Alpha Company captured eight VC during that Search and Clear mission and evacuated them to LZ Thunder.

On 15 August, Alpha Company conducted a combat assault to Ba To, six kilometers southeast of Đức Phổ. Called Operation Golden Valley, this initiative supported the 5th Special Forces Group.

CH-47 Chinooks inserted Alpha Company into the valley near Ba To at 1028 hours in the morning. They moved through streams sometimes thigh deep, the mud and water drenching their socks as it seeped through the metallic eyelets of their combat boots. Using machetes and sweat burning their eyes, they hacked their way through the impenetrable snarl of the steaming jungle and up a mountain unfit for a mountain goat. The thwack of the machetes echoed throughout the column. "The leaches were dropping out of the trees, but I didn't have too much trouble with them," said Ray. At 1108 hours, they detained five VC suspects fourteen years of age and an additional eight VC suspects–all interrogated in the field.

At 1250 hours, they came across an overgrown hedgerow concealing three NVA. The NVA engaged, throwing grenades at elements of 2nd platoon. Hearts pounding, McNown's platoon responded with a barrage of small arms fire and killed two. One escaped, but another element of the 1-20th blocking force captured the enemy soldier. "We really kicked Charlie's butt," said Ray. During that operation, Alpha Company killed eight VC and captured five, quite a change from the trickle of kills in previous operations. They also found weapons, green colored clothing, and important documents describing tactical maneuvers in their Area of Operations. "That was a pretty good catch for this area," said Ray. Their mission complete, Alpha Company set up a NDP at 1940 hours with ambush sites at three locations.

Ray never spoke of the gory details of war or killing enemy combatants. I suppose he thought that my parents did not want to hear the grotesque particulars of combat. He thought it would worry them or compound the horrific thoughts they already had of their son fighting a war in a foreign country. Suffering wounds or worse dying, he thought, would devastate them. The newspapers and TV news programs provided enough of that. Ray kept the content of his letters light. He asked how the family was doing and asked for *more brownies.*

Throughout the AO, humping all day through the dense forest, jungle, and underbrush, then setting up NDPs with ambushes was common throughout the month of August. Tunnel Rats routing the Việt Cộng from their tunnel complexes proved to be challenging as was discerning who was an insurgent in the rural hamlets and who was not. Women and children sometimes harbored weapons, food, and combatants sympathetic to the north. Discretion was the better part of valor, but collateral damage did occur. War is not perfect.

On occasion during sweeps, they could see in the distance rubber plantations with a chateau as a centerpiece, a remnant of French colonial rule. Many of the homes nestled among the rubber trees still occupied families who tended to the estate.

Patrols most every day and night searching for the enemy became the norm. "Sometimes the Doc would pass out pills to keep [us] awake," said Sergeant Matheson. "I don't think they were good for you, but we took them."

Combat does not cease during the evening hours; it knows no specific time of day, no day of the week, no season. A Soldier was "on call" 24/7 with little time to sleep. Soldiers always knew when it was Monday, the day each received the large orange pill to prevent malaria.

It was the middle of the summer, and the mosquitoes were everywhere. "[They] were bad, not as bad as the Kahuku Mountains in Hawaii [where we trained]," said Sergeant Matheson. Of course, malaria was always a potential problem, and Soldiers were strongly encouraged to take the pills. If it wasn't mosquitoes, it was the ants. "They had some mighty big fighting ants."

Ray never experienced a decline in morale in his unit, admirable considering the challenges and discomforts of war and the anti-war protests on the home front. An occasional Dear John letter from a girlfriend at home invaded the psyche of a Soldier and jolted him into a state of depression. Third Platoon spent most of their time in the field, as did the other platoons of Alpha Company. They did not have access to instantaneous news reports nor did they have email or other forms of social media that today provide up to the minute news. On occasion Soldiers would get newspapers from home, two to three weeks old, but they rarely read them. *Stars and Stripes* served the military around the world; most Soldiers read it, but it did not cover anti-war activities like other publications.

John McNown indicated, "The moral held up good in 1968. However, it also depended on the leadership and how [they] reacted to issues. We had good officers and NCOs [in Alpha Company], and they handled issues quickly and thoroughly."

Draftee or volunteer, Soldiers had a sense of duty. They fought for each other, and some fought for the cause. Of those that served in Vietnam, sixty-five percent were volunteers and thirty-five percent draftees. The American fighting Soldier focused on the objective, and little diverted his attention from the mission. Distractions at the very least could result in combat wounds, sometimes serious; at the very worst, death. Each unit (platoon, company, or larger) fought as a Band of Brothers. They looked out for one another.

Yes, there were sporadic minor incidents of dissonance in the ranks, but for the most part, those in leadership positions kept the troops focused on the mission. Such was the case and Ray's experience in Alpha Company.

During subsequent Search and Clear operations for the balance of August, numerous engagements with the Việt Cộng resulted in seven KIA; five CIA, including two NVA; and eighteen VC suspects captured, of which five were female. Choppers evacuated all VC suspects and NVA to LZ Bronco for questioning.

One of these encounters with the VC on the 17th involved Ray's platoon when three opened fire on the Command Post. Returning fire, 3rd platoon effectively maneuvered around the insurgents and killed two, captured one. They also captured an M-1 carbine, a U.S. made M16 with two magazines, and four M26 grenades. This engagement made page three of the 11th Infantry Brigade weekly newsletter, *Trident*. At 1200 hours, they discovered a three-foot-by-three-foot opening to a tunnel, six-foot deep. Members of Ray's platoon searched the tunnel and found remnants of food and signs that weapons were stored there recently.

In the Đức Phổ AO, Alpha Company discovered and destroyed several tunnels, booby traps, and Punji-pits. On one occasion, 19 August, one kilometer northeast of Pho Hoe in the Binh Khe District, an element of Alpha Company discovered a 105 mm artillery round converted to a booby trap. Captain Adams radioed the Engineering Ordinance Disposal (EOD) team for disarming and disposal of the round.

Alpha Company continued to operate in the Pho Hoe area for the next four days with little insurgent contact, each platoon setting up multiple ambush sites in its night defensive positions.

"Sorry I haven't written in a while," Ray wrote in his 20 August letter, "but we've been moving around quite a bit. It's really hard to keep track of time over here. There are no weekends, and every day is just like the rest."

During the latter part of August, Alpha Company operated on both sides of Highway 1 between LZ Thunder and the Brigade Headquarters at LZ Bronco. While one platoon guarded the perimeter of LZ Thunder, the other platoons would be in the bush operating as "snakes" setting up ambushes, "sometimes as many as fifteen ambushes in a night," said McNown. "About sixty men would conduct four or five man ambushes."

Ray loved being with his men in the bush. It was challenging, and there was action. They would hump through the rural areas six to seven kilometers from the main perimeter and return early the next morning, then sleep. They rotated perimeter guard duties with those who set up ambushes. Often times, platoons would conduct sweeps during the day. "What I remember about August besides the heat," said McNown, "was we weren't getting any sleep."

Platoons of the same company did not spend much time together. "It was just the way the war was fought, small unit combat engagements," said McNown.

Sometimes one platoon would be sweeping an area while the other platoons provided security for the base camp. Sometimes two platoons would sweep an area; it just depended on the need.

Like any Soldier, Ray enjoyed the connection with home. "I got your package three days ago," he wrote to Mom. "Keep sending the *Sports Illustrated,* but as far as the candy and cigars go, I really don't need them, because every three days, we get special packages which are sent out to each platoon." Those packages contained cigarettes, candy, cigars, razors, blades, and other miscellaneous items. "If you want to make some brownies or something, that would be great." Ray loved Mom's cooking and welcomed any package from home, as did all Soldiers. The association with home offered a few moments of solitude and a brief distraction from the stress and intensity of military matters.

By the 23rd, all platoons of Alpha Company pulled back to LZ Liz, six and a half kilometers from the coast, conducting security missions for this firebase. Only one engagement took place over the next three days involving 2nd platoon, resulting in one VC KIA wearing an NVA uniform; however, they found five VC bodies.

On the 26th, Ray's platoon enjoyed a day off to rest and refit while 1st and 2nd platoon conducted Search and Clear operations outside the perimeter of Liz. Ray and his platoon were in the bush from the 27th through the 31st conducting patrols and ambushes with no insurgent contact. On the 29th during their sweep, three Klicks west of LZ Bronco, Ray's platoon found a 110 foot tunnel complex, the three-foot-by-three-foot opening heavily camouflaged. In it, they discovered a cache of C-4 explosives and documents. On the morning of the 30th after destroying the tunnel, Helos airlifted the find to LZ Thunder.

By now, Ray had been incountry for about six weeks. He was beginning to feel more comfortable with the men of 3rd platoon and their assigned missions. His honest approach to working with his men, colleagues, and superiors helped establish that sense of trust and rapport that was necessary to solidify bonds among the Soldiers in the unit and be an effective fighting unit.

Ray was not perfect by any means, not immune from making mistakes. He did, however, take ownership of his actions and never made excuses or blamed others for shortfalls in pursuit of his goals or those of the organization.

Ray loved the challenge of a mission. He loved leading, being out front. He liked the feeling of being in control. On Search and Clear missions, more times than not, Ray requested that his platoon be in the lead. In fact, often times he would walk slackman, second in line behind the pointman in his platoon - a dangerous position in the file for a lieutenant, but he believed in leading from the front. He thought it was his responsibility, to show the way–that's what leaders do. He always had a clear vision of his platoon's objective. He fully understood how it fit into the overall strategic mission. He conveyed the details of the mission to his squad leaders and ensured they clearly understood their roles.

Where did he learn these leadership skills and attributes? At the best leader development institution in the world: the United States Military Academy at West Point.

Part II

★ ★ ★

Duty, Honor, Country

Chapter Four

R-DAY

"Duty, Honor, Country –
those three hallowed words reverently dictate what you ought to be,
what you can be, what you will be."
General of the Army Douglas MacArthur
Address to the Corps of Cadets,
12 May 1962

We arrived at Grant Hall at about 9 a.m. It was 1 July 1963, R-Day. Wearing khakis and a short sleeve white polo shirt, Ray said his good-byes. Lacrosse stick in one hand and a small bag of assorted toiletries in the other, Ray was proud to be facing this daunting challenge. Most of America knows West Point, but not the rigors of its academic curriculum or its military training. Attending West Point was a chance of a lifetime, and Ray was looking forward to it. With the same conviction and determination that he faced with academics and athletics in high school, he would do the same at the Academy. He was one of 846 civilians that received an appointment for entrance to this prestigious institution.

R-Day was Reception Day for Cadet Candidates, the first day of Beast Barracks. Those that survived the next two months would become Fourth Classmen, more commonly called Plebes, or as many upperclassmen might say, a substandard human being beneath the Navy "goat," that is, on the sociological spectrum of mammalogy.

"Beast" was designed to siphon out all that was civilian and transform a home spun citizen into a cadet, albeit, hour-by-hour, day-by-day. It was psychologically stressful and physically demanding, more than you can imagine–no excuses for falling short of its carefully designed and uniformly implemented curriculum.

From the moment Cadet Candidates passed through the Sally Port, they became a part of a highly disciplined, rapid paced, extremely organized whirlwind of events and undertakings. First, barbers stripped Cadet Candidates of their hair in a fashion that took all of five minutes. Clad in white T-shirts, gray shorts, black socks, and black shoes, civilian cadre measured Cadet Candidates for their uniforms. Nurses inoculated them, not once, but several times. Cadet Cadre supervised the physical fitness test that included pull-ups, push-ups, sit-ups, standing broad jump, and a kneeling basketball throw.

Cadet Candidates responded four ways to a question or statement made by an upperclassman: "Yes Sir," "No Sir," "No excuse Sir," or "Sir, I do not understand." How did a New Cadet know this? From their first unfortunate encounter with the "Man in the Red Sash." He was a member of the upper class cadre that would direct the indoctrination of all Cadet Candidates to West Point's traditions and spearhead the transition from civilian to cadet. If you "messed-up," you reported to the Man in the Red Sash. Just listen closely, follow instructions, and, well, "suck it up."

If you thought this was a summer camp, forget it. Those who arrived with guitars, golf clubs, and a suitcase full of clothing (for all seasons), were quickly divested of their country club ways. Cadet Candidates received everything they needed from shoulder belts to waist belts, from poncho to poncho liner, from white undershirts to white boxer shorts. If you were partial to Fruit of the Loom jockey shorts, you were out of luck. As they approached the supply line, they were told, "The red tag goes on the green bag, the white tag on your belt, and the blue tag on your valuables." Uniformity and conformity were tradition at the Academy; no room for individuality.

The bombardment of orders and instructions was overwhelming and often intimidating. Suffer the ridicule of harassment if you forgot a command. Do not ask questions–the cadre told you all you needed to know. Do not volunteer for anything, either. Better to remain under a cloak of anonymity.

On the day of arrival, they learned the finer points of marching, turning, standing at attention with feet spread at a forty-five degree angle, and saluting, some better than others.

Ray as well as all Cadet Candidates learned to "Brace" immediately upon arrival, the more bulging the wrinkles in the neck and chin the better. Upperclassmen would say, "*Suck in your chin, smack,*" just another form of discipline and harassment for the fledgling Cadet Candidates.

Peering curiously through the "Sally Port," my parents, Sandra, and I could see them negotiate left turns, right turns, about-faces. Some would stumble.

Very few were precise. We could hear upperclassmen shouting commands, like roll your hips forward, shoulders back, suck in your gut, and forward march; not that left foot, "bean-head"; your other left, when a Cadet Candidate began marching with his right foot.

We would not see Ray until the end of the day and only a distant visual at that, as the Cadet Candidates marched to Trophy Point for the swearing-in ceremony. We were lucky that day to be able to take a picture of him marching in lock step with the others clad in gray slacks and white shirt with barren gray epaulets. On occasion, some would fall out of step, but overall, after seven long hours of hazing, collecting clothing, and learning the basics of marching, they stayed in step. The expressions on their faces ranged from pure exhaustion to *"What the hell did I get myself into."* One parent called his son's name as he marched by, but the mask of a look on all their faces was as solid as the granite that veneered the surrounding buildings; a tell-tale sign of their state of mind.

Upon arriving at Trophy Point, the swearing-in ceremony began. *Repeat after me*, echoed throughout the Cadet Candidate ranks,

> I do solemnly swear that I will support the Constitution of the United Sates and bear true allegiance to the national government; that I will maintain and defend the sovereignty of the United States, paramount to any and all allegiance, sovereignty, or fealty I may owe to any State, county, or country whatsoever; and that I will at all times obey the legal orders of my superior officers, and the rules and articles governing the Armies of the United States.

At the conclusion of the ceremony, they marched back to their barracks first to eat dinner and then begin the arduous chore of learning to be a New Cadet. The week after the swearing in ceremony Ray said, "We've been drilling, receiving more equipment, going to lectures, folding laundry while getting the millions of things we were issued into our lockers."

Tradition required "racks" (beds) to be made using hospital corners and tight enough to bounce a quarter one inch in the air when dropped from a height of three feet. Strict protocols dominated the essence of room organization and cleanliness: clothing folded and organized, drawers opened for inspection in a prescribed manner, top drawer opened six inches, and the bottom drawer, nine inches. Rooms so spotless it would have infuriated Mr. Clean; a droplet of water in the sink was as bad as a speck of dust on the blinds.

Making a bed or maintaining sleeping quarters to an exact set of specifications sounds childish and mundane at best. Today, thinking back on my experience as a Cadet Candidate, I recall the movie *Karate Kid.* "Wash on … wash off." Before a cadet or Soldier can advance to the more sophisticated endeavors of soldiering, he or she must learn to perfect the basics through disciplined thought and action. Perfect one task, then take on another, and then another. Routine and a process orientation enabled cadets and future Soldiers to sharpen their skills in a seamless manner.

Relentless hazing tested Cadets Candidates' ability to act under pressure, listen, and follow instructions. Brigadier General Richard G. Stilwell, former Commandant of Cadets, said, "If you can't learn to obey orders explicitly, you will never be able to give orders properly," perhaps a reasonable justification for the intensity of harassment.

Ray recalled his first week of Beast Barracks in a 6 July letter to my parents. "The first day was about the worst, but it really wasn't that bad. After I left you, we went and checked in as they measured us for uniforms. We took two physical fitness tests and were issued a duffle bag. We were then brought into the main area where we met the upperclassmen. They started running us around getting equipment, drilling, and bracing."

Beast indoctrinated Cadet Candidates into military life; eliminated arrogance, cockiness, and self-centered attitudes. Beast instilled structure, discipline, and teamwork in all that Cadet Candidates did; that is how, in part; a leader accomplishes the mission and saves lives in combat.

Ray learned how to carry his M-14 rifle and perform the myriad of rifle positions: present arms, order arms, and parade rest. The proper name for a rifle is "weapon." If a cadre member caught a Cadet Candidate calling it a gun, he was told to "brace" and repeat ten times, holding his groin with one hand while holding his rifle with the other; "This is my rifle. This is my gun. This is for shooting. This is for fun."

They moved at the doubled-time *everywhere* with high expectations of being on time for formations, uniforms neatly pressed, "gig-line" straight, belt buckle polished, shoes "spit" shined, and gloves as white as a newly fallen flake of snow. If there was the slightest aberration, cadre strafed the Candidate and his roommate with harassment. Roommates checked each other off prior to formations, another useful expectation of Beast.

At the mess hall, class designated seats dominated table protocol. First Classmen sat at the head of the table. Second Classmen sat in the middle, and so on. New Cadets sat, of course, at the end of the table, and each had a prescribed responsibility.

New Cadets sat on the front six inches of their chair and ate a "square meal," raising the fork or spoon from the plate directly vertical to a height no greater than horizontal with the mouth and at a right angle, slowly bringing the food directly inward toward the mouth, returning the utensil to the plate in the same fashion. Uniformity required the West Point Coat of Arms with the helmet of "Athena" on their plate be positioned at 12 o'clock and knives placed at the top of the plate parallel to the edge of the table, blade facing inward. Always!

Ray did not mind the structure or the discipline–he could do, however, without the harassment. "This is really a great place and I love it up here, so far. Only two things bother me. We get very little to eat. This is because we have to take bites no bigger than our smallest fingernail. We must eat while bracing and sitting on the front one-third of our chair and by the time we get all the food passed out, we have very little time to eat. I've lost seven pounds already after one week and my ribs are showing."

"The other thing I don't like is shower formation. All nine men in our squad line up and brace up against the wall. The upperclassmen yell and scream at us until we sweat through our bathrobe; then we are permitted to take a shower. You really don't listen and it doesn't bother me."

"Bugle Notes," otherwise known as the Plebe Bible, contained a wealth of information about West Point, Fourth Class customs and traditions, West Point songs, and Plebe knowledge called "poop" that was an essential part of Beast Barracks and Plebe year.

Upper class cadre members loved to harass Plebes, particularly at meals. "Cadet Candidate Enners, how's a cow?" In a commanding voice, Ray would respond, "*Sir, she walks, she talks, she's full of chalk, the lacteal fluid extracted from the female of the bovine species is highly prolific to the nth degree.*" An upperclassman would reprimand Ray if he missed one word or did not know it with "*Sit up, too slow,*" until such time as the upperclassman said so, he could not eat. Or, he would likely not eat for the rest of the meal. Ray knew his "poop"; he made sure of that.

"Clothing formations" tested your calm and resilience under pressure. A company of New Cadets would fall out into the quadrangle, and an upper class cadre would name a uniform, from gym clothing to dress whites. New Cadets would have two minutes to run back into their rooms, dress in that uniform, ensure their room was neat, and "report back" to the quadrangle for inspection. It was impossible, but that was the point of it all. Maintaining your cool under pressure was a desirable trait for a leader who in five years would lead a platoon in combat.

It was 14 July, two weeks since R-Day. "Everything is starting to fit into a pattern," said Ray. "During the week we have drill, conditioning exercises, manual of arms, and several lectures on customs, traditions, and etiquette. We're moving every minute, though. We have been getting more to eat lately, thanks to our Table Commandant's girlfriend. She told him to take it easy on us, so he is. For this we all had to write her a thank you note, which we did last night."

Ray as well as all New Cadets studied and embraced the Honor System and the Honor Code. A cadet will not "lie, cheat, steal, or tolerate those who do." Integrity is the very essence of cadet life and morals by which an Army Officer lives. If character is the very foundation of leadership, then integrity is the guiding light. It is also the basis of trust, the foundation of a team, which is necessary to have a cohesive and effective military unit.

The concept of the Honor System was started by Sylvanus Thayer when he was superintendent from 1817-1833 and formalized under Superintendent General Douglas MacArthur in 1919. In an attempt to develop the "whole man" philosophy, MacArthur was not only interested in leadership development, academic and military excellence, and athletic ability; he was interested in developing the character of the individual. He established a Cadet Honor Committee composed of cadets to oversee and administer all aspects of the Honor System.

Day-in, day-out New Cadets followed a prescribed schedule of activities that familiarized them with cadet life. From reveille to taps, they recited "plebe poop," attended classes, and learned basic military skills. The highlight of Beast was the all-night bivouac during the last week.

As the upperclassmen returned from leave or Army Orientation Training (AOT), the new academic year began, and for Ray, it was the beginning of Plebe year. Company B-1, the 1st Regiment, had a tradition of being the toughest regiment in the Corps. This would be Ray's home for the next four years. Ray was up at 0600 hours and to bed no earlier than 2400 hours–a full day of classes five days during the week and half-day on Saturday occupied his time. Formations for meals and thirty minutes to eat kept him on schedule; and in between, reciting "plebe poop" for the upperclassmen kept Ray on his toes. How many gallons in Lusk Reservoir, smack? Ray responded, *"90.2 million gallons, Sir, when the water is flowing over the spillway."*

You might think all of this discipline and shelling Plebes with harassment was absurd. Having graduated from West Point, I can tell you that it taught me how to adapt to changing situations, how to deal with complex and diverse issues and handle stress. The Academy's philosophy is that no one can predict the future, particularly what wars will be fought, under what conditions or rules of engagement, and where. A cadet and Army Officer must learn to adapt both on and off the battlefield. That is the brutal reality of military life. An Army Officer also has to be able to handle stress under life threatening conditions. This was just a way of getting prepared.

West Point was a journey of learning, a journey of growing; a complex set of beliefs that formulate an ethos of behavior, not just for the four years at the Academy, but also for life. The Academy's methodology planned nearly every minute of the day, for a reason. One leadership principle stood out to me. Because of the rigorous schedule, up at 0600 hours and to bed sometimes at midnight with countless responsibilities in between, there were many opportunities during the day to experience failure. West Point taught me that when I fell short of expectations or a desired outcome, I assessed the situation, developed a course of action, and moved ahead. There was no time for blaming, lamenting, or retreating. Blaming is for the weak, lamenting is for the emotional, and retreating is dishonorable. The Academy's method of education and training taught me to meet challenges head-on; first understand it, next formulate a plan, and then act.

The rigorous routine continued. At times Ray cut the cake or pie at dinner. He fabricated a round six inch diameter template and carried it in the inside of his hat. On the surface of the template, he marked a center point and ten equal divisions radiating to the edge so that he could cut ten equal slices; no room for error. If improperly done, upperclassmen shelled out more harassment. Hey "bean-head," how many names on Battle Monument? Ray would reply, *"2,230 names, Sir."*

If you performed well during the meals, the Table Commandant might allow "big bites," but otherwise, you ate "small bites," not near enough to fill the stomach of a cadet constantly on the run. Plebes served drinks and ensured there was sufficient food on the table for everyone. Ray memorized the menu for each meal, should the upperclassmen want to know.

The entire Corps of Cadets, more than 2,500 strong, ate their meals at the same time in Washington Hall. Thirty minutes to eat a meal may seem like a challenge, but Washington Hall orchestrated the service of each meal similar to a Michelin rated three star dining establishment; food arrived at each table within minutes of sitting down, family style. The bustle of activity would impress anyone in the profession of culinary arts–waiters moving briskly through the maze of tables to deliver food.

During the fall of the year, cadets paraded each Saturday, weather permitting, and on special occasions during the week (but rarely). As the Plebes lined up in the quadrangles and checked each other off, you could hear a moaning plea to the Norwegian god Odin. A successful plea would bring rain and cancel the parade. Oooooo-din, Oooooo-din, Oooooo-din. Rarely did it work.

With knees slightly bent, Ray learned the art of standing still, dead still, over an extended period. On occasion in extreme hot weather, a cadet might collapse. If you were on either side of the "fallen one," it was your job to pick him up and help him along.

There was excitement on the grounds as the football season approached. Plebes held pep rallies, sang songs like "On Brave Old Army Team" or "Black, Gold, Gray", raising the level of enthusiasm for the Army team by the entire Corp of Cadets, commonly known at the 12th man.

Since Ray played football in high school, he was eligible and a ripe candidate to practice with the "150 pound" football team prior to the official season. What a great sport. On the Thursday before a Saturday game, each varsity player had to "make weight," that is, weigh no more than 154 pounds. West Point was one of the few teams to compete in this contest of Mighty Mites, in addition to Navy, Penn, Cornell, and Princeton. Because the Plebe players were usually taller and heavier, they would make strong competition for the varsity team during drills and scrimmages. It was an advantage for Ray, as he could sit on training tables and eat as much as he wanted. It was "150 pound" football where he met Larry Izzo, nicknamed "Homer," and convinced him to try out for off-season lacrosse.

Larry was from Greenlawn, Long Island. At Harborfields High School, he was an excellent athlete making the All-Suffolk County football team in his senior year, as did Ray. After graduation from the Academy, Larry served with the 101st Airborne Division in Vietnam. Larry received the Bronze Star with Valor and Purple Heart for his service. He later led a unit with the 82nd Airborne Division during the liberation of Grenada. He taught physics at West Point. After serving twenty-three years in the service, he transitioned to private business where he was CEO of Calpine Power Services, then a division of Enron.

"In typical unselfish fashion, Ray spent hours and hours teaching me how to pass and catch," said Larry. They would practice lacrosse on the weekends, mainly because they did not have dates. "I was indebted to Ray for life," he said. Larry made the Plebe team and played lacrosse all four years as a mid-fielder.

Army-Navy football was approaching. A trip to Municipal Stadium, named John F. Kennedy Stadium the next year, was a great chance for Ray to see the outside world after being isolated for the past five months. Ray and the entire Corps took the train from the West Point station on the level of the Hudson River to Philly via several stops. The Army mule accompanied the Corps as well. My mom, dad, sister, and I met Ray in Philly after the game.

"The game of 1963" was widely publicized, a contest that featured junior quarterback Rollie Stichweh and Heisman Trophy winner Roger Staubach. Coached by Paul Dietzel, Army entered the game with a lifetime record of 30 wins to Navy's 28, and 5 ties. The score toward the end of the game was Navy 21, Army 15. With only minutes left, Rollie recovered an on-side kick and marched the team to within two yards of Navy's goal line. In a stadium filled with 106,000 people, the crowd was cheering so loud that Rollie knew the team could not hear his signals. He raised his hands—not once, but twice—to quiet the roaring crowd. The referee neglected to stop the clock in an attempt to quiet the crowd and time ran out. The final score stood, 21-15. Army avenged their prior year loss and bounced back that next year. They beat nationally ranked Navy, 11-8.

As fall gave way to winter, "gloom period" set in. For nearly five months everywhere Ray turned, there was gray: gray buildings, gray walkways, gray sky, and gray uniforms. And, that cold northern breeze screaming its way through the Hudson Highlands made him want to hibernate.

Nininger Hall offered some reprieve from the brutal winters. There, Ray could socialize with friends unhampered by upper class hazing, listen to music, and commiserate over the challenges of Plebe life. Once he left Nininger Hall, he was once again subject to the strict disciplines of Academy life. On one occasion, an upperclassman stopped Ray and asked, "What do Plebes rank?" Ray "popped off," *"Sir, the Superintendent's dog, the Commandant's cat, the waiters in the mess hall, the 'Hell Cats' [marching band], the Generals in the Air Force, and all the Admirals in the whole damned Navy."* The harassment continued.

Christmas was just a few days away. Upperclassmen scrambled to get home to friends and family; not the Plebes, however. Ray and the rest of the Fourth Classmen would spend Christmas at West Point.

My parents, Sandra, and I made our way up the Palisades Parkway to spend Christmas Day with Ray, which included a dinner in Washington Hall. He was in good spirits, but exhausted from the academic rigors and Plebe challenges. Nonetheless, he took it in stride.

Ray's class was the last class to spend Christmas at West Point.

Turmoil was brewing in the South Vietnamese Government. Buddhist protested the religious persecution of the Diem regime and high-ranking military officials became displeased with Diem's rule. On 1 November 1963, Dương Văn Minh led a coup and seized power. Diem and his brother Ngo Dinh Nhu were murdered.

Earlier in the year, the Army of the Republic of Vietnam (ARVN) suffered a major defeat at the hands of the Việt Cộng at Ap Bac, southwest of Saigon. President Johnson's advisors deduced that if South Vietnam fell to the Communists the balance of Southeast Asia would fall. Former President Dwight Eisenhower called it the "Domino Theory." In a top-secret National Security Action Memorandum (NSAM) 273 Johnson said, "It remains the central objective of the United States in South Vietnam to assist the people and Government of that country to win their contest against the externally directed and supported Communist conspiracy."

By the end of 1963, American troop levels exceeded 16,000. It consisted mostly of Special Forces (Green Beret) Soldiers who trained the ARVN. America was moving closer to an all-out military conflict.

For about four weeks during the winter, Ray played off-season lacrosse in the field house. The team worked on conditioning, stick handling, dodging, ground balls, and fast breaks. Artificial turf was not available at the time, so the dirt floor in the field house sufficed, particularly when they played the first game of the season against Yale, and snow blanketed the Academy grounds. Ray welcomed off-season lacrosse. It was a great stress release.

Spring was within sight, and that would bring welcome improvements in the quality of Ray's life. Lacrosse was in season, and that meant sitting at training tables during meals: no bracing, no square meals, plenty of food, and "big bites." That put a smile on Ray's face as it did all Plebe athletes who played intercollegiate sports.

According to NCAA rules at the time, all college freshmen had to play freshman sports. They were not eligible for the varsity squad, better known as the "A" team, in the vernacular of West Point. Ray would make new friends on the lacrosse team: Ed Sullivan, recruited from Baltimore; Glynn Hale from Kentucky; and he would see Chris Pettit again.

I remember making the trip to West Point on Saturdays with my family, enough food in the car to feed an army. After the game Ray would invite his friends over to the car to eat, and eat they did. Mom spent days making lasagna, brownies, and bread. Plenty of orange juice quenched their thirst.

Under Coach John Orlando, it was a great season. Ray formed a special bond with teammates Chris, Ed, Glynn, Mike Spinello and Larry Izzo that would last for the next three years and well after graduation.

It was June Week 1964, and with academic rigors behind him, Ray looked forward to the parade the day before the Class of 1964 graduated. It was after that parade he and all the Plebes were "recognized" by the upperclassmen, an unforgettable ceremony in the quadrangle and historic triumph of Plebe year. Each upperclassman in his company shook his hand. He was now a Yearling, a Third Classman, and officially rose to a level higher than the Superintendent's dog and Commandant's cat; one stripe and a gold Athena helmet clad insignia adorned each epaulet of his summer whites, and one black stripe on each lower sleeve added to his dress grays.

The Greek Goddess Pallas Athena captures the essence of the Academy. The daughter of Zeus (in Greek mythology), Athena represents wisdom, learning, courage, inspiration, and military victory. With the utmost respect afforded to Greece, she only took part in wars that defended the state. The helmet of Athena along with the shield, bald eagle, and thirteen arrows representing the thirteen original states plays a pivotal role in every aspect of West Point's culture and the branding of the Academy.

The Class of 1967 embraced their class motto, "None Will Surpass," and it became a measure that they lived by, not only at the Academy, but also in their personal and professional lives thereafter. As Plebes, the class became close; bonds strengthened as the years went on.

Ray took a deep breath; on to the next challenge. He loved West Point. He departed for home on 30 days leave and then reported to Camp Buckner for seven weeks of summer training.

Chapter Five

Iggy Inch

"The one quality that can be developed by
studious reflection and practice
is the leadership of men."

Dwight D. Eisenhower
USMA 1915

Summer leave ended and Ray anxiously reported to Camp Buckner. Tucked away in the mountains southwest of West Point, this training base would be his introduction to becoming a Soldier. Buckner sat in the midst of oak and maple trees, wooden barracks and Lake Popolopen, the grounds used for both training and recreation.

During the next seven weeks Ray was introduced to many of the Army's combat arms, Artillery, Infantry, Engineers, Signal Corps, and Armor, but the majority of the training was focused on the capabilities, limitations, and methods of deployment of infantry weapons, squad and platoon tactics and skills, and day and night navigation.

Using a pugil stick with the approximate weight of a rifle and bayonet, Ray learned close order fighting in the sawdust pits. Using medieval gladiator type moves, this training taught cadets to throw a blow, take a blow, and acclimate themselves to violent situations. For hours, they would twist and turn their classmates to the ground, simulating close order hand-to-hand fighting.

He fired the M-14 rifle, .45 caliber pistol, and M60 machine gun on the firing range. He learned how to dissemble and re-assemble hand held weapons. He tossed hand grenades, fired anti-tank weapons, learned survival techniques, and experienced night patrolling as part of the "Recondo" (Reconnaissance and Commando) phase. Training emphasized confidence building, physical conditioning, and establishing a philosophy of teamwork.

These skills are critical for an officer in the infantry, particularly the capability and deployment of weapons. "A leader must master the essential skills, weapons, and equipment of the men he leads. How else will he know if they are being employed and maintained properly?" said classmate Glynn Hale based on his experience in Vietnam. "Knowing how to load and fire an M60 doesn't come close. He has to know how to field strip it, perform maintenance, identify and fire at different rates of fire, and how to employ the guns under various conditions." For the Yearlings Camp Buckner was merely the beginning of their training on weaponry and tactics.

Glynn, an "Army Brat", lived in Fort Knox, Kentucky, prior to entering West Point. During his combat tour in Vietnam (June 1968 through January 1970), he served in the 2nd Battalion, 506th Infantry Regiment, 101st Airborne Infantry in both the I Corps and III Corps Tactical Zones. He received three Silver Stars, two Bronze Stars with Valor, and two Purple Hearts for his acts of valor as a rifle platoon leader, "recon" platoon leader, and rifle company commander. Most important was earning the Combat Infantryman's Badge (CIB) awarded to infantry Soldiers who served in a combat zone. It is an award "of which I am most proud and humbled," said Glynn. He retired as a Colonel after twenty-four years of service to the nation.

At Camp Buckner, the cadre also talked at great lengths about what it took to be a leader in combat. Ed Sullivan recalled, "One of the principles that was taught was mission comes first, followed by welfare of your troops. If you lose sight of either one, you will not be successful. The problem solving and perseverance, the grit and the grind," he went on to say, "built character, an underpinning that allowed us to take on whatever it might be that came our way."

Classmate Harry Rothmann said, "I think you can teach leadership, but the best leaders are those that understand people. Leadership is more a feeling of the heart than it is studying leadership principles. I think as human beings we understand that, if we step back and think about it." Harry felt that Ray thought the same way he did.

As part of the personal development process, the Army has an Officer Efficiency Rating (OER) system whereby the senior officer rates the subordinate officer. "Too many officers are always looking up, and their loyalties are only to their superiors," said Harry. He was convinced that more focus by the leader should be on developing stronger "peer to peer" and "[superior] to subordinate" relationships, creating an environment where professional connections can flourish. "Leadership is looking at people in a positive way and developing trust. Also, treating people respectfully gains trust." Harry felt Ray would agree with that. "I think that motivated him," said Harry.

Upon receiving the Sylvanus Thayer Award at West Point in 2003, General Gordon R. Sullivan (USA Ret.) spoke to the cadets about trust as a requisite of leadership. "A Soldier's trust–this is what I think Soldiering is all about, and I believe it is an officer's duty to ensure all in his or her command know that the foundation upon which all of this rests is what this place [West Point] is all about: service performed selflessly, and mutual trust and respect between leader and the led."

Buckner was not all training. On the weekends, cadets could have visitors. They would invite their "Drags", cadet slang for dates. It was downtime, time to spend with friends, time to swim in the lake, boat, or just relax. A Relais et Châteaux resort it was, compared to the pressure cooker and regimented environment of plebe year, that is.

"I tried to call tonight but you [Mom] weren't home. We leave for Recondo tomorrow at 4 a.m. They told us not to expect to get more than seven hours sleep for the whole week." During Recondo Ray experienced survival training, all night reconnaissance patrols, and plenty of running and forced marches. During the mountaineering phase, he repelled from a sixty-five foot high cliff. A cadre member prepared "raider stew" comprised of turtle, beans, snake, and rabbit; all fresh, really fresh. He demonstrated how to strip the skin from a snake. The highlight was the "Slide for Life" on the last day of the 79-hour "Recondo" course. Ray climbed the seventy foot tower, grabbed on to a trolley attached to a thin cable, and slid to within a height of ten feet above the lake. He let go. It was a thrill, a rush, as I personally remember the event during my Yearling summer as a cadet.

Yearling summer ended on a high note. Then Ray and his classmates reluctantly returned to the Academy grounds for Reorganization Week, five days to prepare for the new academic year. Back to the grind. Ray's course load included Chemistry, Western World Literature, Psychology of Leading, French, Calculus and Differential Equations, History of Russia and the Middle East, Roles and Missions of the Armed Forces, and Physics. For the fall and spring semesters, Ray took 42 academic credit hours.

Classroom size was small, ranging from 12 to 15 cadets. The ratio of students to faculty was about 8:1, emphasizing a classroom environment of discussion, not lecture. Each student was encouraged to speak up and often took the lead in presenting solutions to problems and articulating new ideas. Grades posted in

Sally Ports connected to the barracks provided cadets with a weekly understanding of where they stood in each course.

Harry Rothmann roomed with Ray for the first half of the Yearling academic year. They got to know each other well and became good friends. "He was never judgmental about people," said Harry. "I never heard him say a bad word about anybody. He understood that we all had strengths and weaknesses—and always sought the good in people."

He also recalled that Ray worked like a son-of-a-bitch to pass math and physics, physics in particular. "Math was a little easier", said Harry. "You had the formulas in the big green book." If you studied that and put your nose to the grindstone, you could pretty much get through it. All Ray needed was to know where to get the information.

"The more difficult subject was physics because it was applied physics," Harry said. "Ray didn't have the same physics in high school that I had. That's where Larry Izzo came in to help. Ray was determined to study and achieve in those two courses. He tried as hard as he possibly could. He put his nose to the grindstone. For physics, it was difficult. But, what he exhibited on the athletic field and other endeavors at West Point, he also did in academics."

There is statue of General Sedgwick on the grounds at West Point cast from cannons captured by the VI Corps, which he commanded during the Civil War. There is a tradition tied to the statue. If a cadet is deficient in a subject, and he spins the rowel spurs on General Sedgwick's boots before a major exam, it will bring good luck. Harry and Ray did just that. At 1 a.m. on the day of the exam, they donned their full dress uniform, under arms, stole out to the statue, and spun the spurs. Ray passed the exam that day.

Chris Pettit echoed the same about how hard Ray worked. In a eulogy Chris wrote, "At times the academic road was particularly rough for him. Yet, through extraordinary personal effort, he managed to overcome this hurdle where others would have stumbled." Chris admired Ray's "twinkling wit" and "never give up" spirit.

Ray was shy around women. Harry Rothmann remembers one funny incident that happened Yearling year. "In those days we lived on the first floor of Old South Barracks," said Harry. Old South Barracks was on Thayer Road at the time when it was open to pedestrian and vehicle traffic. On weekends Harry would say, "Ray, let's talk to some girls." Harry would open the huge window, and as the girls walked by, they would flirt with them. "[Ray] was not very good at flirting," Harry recalled. "He was very shy with women."

Another Gloom Period hung over West Point - damp, dark, and gray - but Christmas was coming, and the thought of spending it this year at home on Long Island pleased Ray.

By the time Ray became a Yearling, the Vietnam Conflict was heating up, and the news from Southeast Asia began to invade the vocabulary of cadet life. Secretary of Defense McNamara prepared document 201 on 5 June 1964 for President Johnson that outlined a South Vietnam Action Program. It included expanding the U.S. and South Vietnamese initiatives in eight critical provinces, initially adding U.S. personnel from within South Vietnam and shifting forces to and within Hawaii, Guam, Philippines, and Okinawa. The long-term strategy was still unclear. Would it be a strategy of containment using counterinsurgency? Would it be a protracted war of attrition? History showed that waging war on foreign soil required popular support. Alternatively, would the United States focus on destroying the "center of gravity," North Vietnam?

While the United States debated a course of action, General Võ Nguyên Giáp of the North Vietnamese Army rearmed the Việt Cộng and sent additional North Vietnamese soldiers to the south, about 12,000 in 1964.

He also directed terrorist activities against U.S. advisors and military installations. General Giáp made use of the newly constructed trail on the Laotian and Cambodian border to infiltrate the south with communist troops and supplies. A major supply route was born, the Hồ Chí Minh trail. He made two major mistakes, though; one, he directed insurgent activities at American Soldiers, and two, he permitted reckless bombings of civilian buses, marketplaces, hotels, and other public buildings. This turned the southern populace against the Việt Cộng. Still, the Việt Cộng held their own and, in fact, by the end of 1964, they formed their first operational combat division by combining two regiments, the 271st and the 272nd.

By the end of 1964, while the South Vietnamese forces increased their strength to over 500,000 men, President Johnson continued to reaffirm Americas support for South Vietnam. In a National Security Action Memorandum (NSAM) 273 he said the U.S. objective was to assist South Vietnam in its "contest against the externally directed and supported communist conspiracy." President Johnson initiated an informal declaration of war (not a legal declaration) against North Vietnam. The United States and the Army of the Republic of Vietnam (ARVN) would meet the Việt Cộng and North Vietnamese Army on the battlefield using counter-insurgency tactics.

By year's end, 216 American Soldiers arrived at Dover Air Force Base, Delaware, in flag draped coffins, while 23,000 U.S. military personnel supported the effort incountry.

It was Yearling year that Ray received his nickname, Iggy. Ed Sullivan remembered, "In those days playing lacrosse as Yearlings, we became a part of a team where everyone had a nickname. There were nicknames like the Bird, Bomber, and the Duck; the Tree and Bork." Chris Pettit went to high school with an individual whose last name was the same as Ed's name. His nickname was "Suell." That became Ed's nickname.

Who gave Ray the nickname "Iggy" had always been a mystery. I knew why and where the name came from but not who. In the early sixties, a cartoon character named "Iggy Inch" from the "Little Lulu" comic strip that frequently appeared in the newspapers was popular with young girls and boys. He had very short hair, as did Ray, even in high school, which was highly unusual at the time, considering many men supported the longer locks custom.

As I dug deeper, I discovered that Chris Pettit and his wife Mary Anne did the honors. Mary Anne recalled, "I remember the night; we were just hanging out. I believe it was after Plebe year. I was rubbing Ray's head and I said, 'I just love this. Your head doesn't feel like this, Chris.' Chris went over to Ray and touched his head, and he said, 'Oh my god, it feels just like Iggy's.' It came from just fooling around and the way his hair felt. We would touch his head, and he didn't seem to mind. That's the funny thing."

Harry Rothmann remembered, "His nickname started off slowly, and by junior year, it was used fairly frequently."

The name Iggy was born that would follow him through West Point and beyond. Ray's friends still to this day fondly use the name Iggy when referring to Ray.

The spring lacrosse season was approaching. It was Ray's passion, as it was my parents' passion watching him play. They would not only travel to West Point for the games, but to the Baltimore area as well.

Ray played Attack as he did in high school, and as Coach Jim "Ace" Adams said, "Ray was a solid mainstay of the offensive array of the Army team."

What midfielder Glynn Hale remembered about Iggy was not his skills. It was "his work ethic, determination, and team focus. He knew when to be silent and just do it, and when to provide the encouragement we lesser skilled players needed. He led, whether he knew it or not, by his personal example and commitment to the team. It came easy to him, because that [was] who he was."

Ed Sullivan, a midfielder on the team, said, "People looked up to Ray, at least on Attack, as the standard you would strive for. In those days, [several] offensive players hung their stick out, more flat than vertical. Ray was one of the first, maybe next to Jimmy Lewis at the Naval Academy, who carried his stick vertical all of the time to protect the ball. It caused others to say, 'Oh, that's really what we should be doing.' It is a small thing, but by leading by example and doing it in a better way, people emulated that."

West Point finished the season that year with eight wins and four losses, including an 18-7 loss to Navy. Navy won the USILA National Championship that year. Ray had 10 goals and 11 assists. That determination he exhibited in everything he did earned him the L.B. Crandall Award many times during the season, for the most "loose balls" recovered.

It was June Week, 1965. Ray's final exams were over and the graduating class would soon receive their diplomas. Ray replaced his gold Athena class insignia with Gray and added an additional stripe to his epaulet. He also added an additional stripe to both sleeves of his cadet gray uniform. He was now a Second Classman.

Ray headed home on a thirty day summer leave. After spending time with friends and playing summer lacrosse at Jones Beach, he reported to Fort Hood, Texas, as a part of West Point's Army Orientation Training (AOT) program. He was assigned to Company A, 2-13th, 1st Armor Division, learning the tactical capabilities of the Armor profession. Customary for this assignment, NCO and enlisted personnel would not call him Lieutenant Enners; they would call him Mr. Enners.

Living in the Bachelor's Officers Quarters (BOQ) was great. Ray said, "I have my own room in a BOQ and a maid who cleans the room and makes the bed." Such is life away from West Point.

He went on to say, "There are a lot of good looking girls around here, too. I took one of them out a couple of times and found out her dad was a brigadier general and won the Medal of Honor in WW II. He was very nice, and I enjoyed talking to him."

Soon, it was September 1965, back to school, back to reality.

Chapter Six

NO TURNING BACK

"What the modern officer needs,
aside from all technical abilities, is character,
or so at least West Point believes,
and that is what it gives its cadets."

Stephen E. Ambrose, Author

Iggy was a "Cow," an odd name for a cadet in his third year at the Academy. Its origin unknown, the most popular explanation dates back to the 1920s when Academy regulations permitted cadets to take only one leave per year, beginning in the summer before their third academic year. As they arrived at the West Point train station on the Hudson River, and the wave of cadets climbed the hill heading for the Plain, a bystander metaphorically said, "The cows are coming home." The name stuck.

There were 730 "and a butt" days until graduation–no turning back, not that Ray wanted to.

His course load was heavy, over 42 credit hours for the year; Electricity, commonly called "juice", Mechanics of Fluids, Introduction to Law, Mechanics of Solids, Political Philosophy and Combined Employment of the Combined Arms Team.

His nickname Iggy became more and more popular. Mary Anne Pettit went to Cortland State just four hours from West Point. Every weekend she would bring a blind date for Iggy. "Everybody loved him," she said. "He was so easy going, and they all thanked me." Upper class cadets would meet their Drags at Grant Hall on Thayer Road. Dating back to 1852, Grant Hall, known as the Old Cadet Mess Hall, served as the dining hall for the Corps of Cadets. It was replaced by Washington Hall and demolished in 1930 to make way for the construction of the then Grant Hall. It is a prestigious building with plush chairs, and adorning the walls are artistically cast oil paintings of 5-star generals George Marshall, Douglas MacArthur, Dwight Eisenhower, Henry (Hap) Arnold, and Omar Bradley.

After rendezvousing, cadets and their Drags would walk around the Academy grounds, attend functions, or just "hang-out." Public Display of Affection (PDA) was strictly prohibited; no handholding or kissing. There was one authorized location for this, "Flirtation Walk," a dirt trail just below the level of the Plain on the north and east side of the grounds. It even included "Kissing Rock," a welcomed stop along the trail.

On weekends, the other alternative was Snuffy's ten miles from West Point–the legal limit for alcohol–where Iggy could get the finest burger in the area and a beer. It was a pub of sorts, where good friends and good cheer came together.

The war in South Vietnam continued to escalate with the U.S. bombings of North Vietnam. This prompted Hanoi to send additional grounds troops to the south. The monthly draft call in America increased to meet the demands of the war. Off the coast of North Vietnam, the U.S. Navy increased its aircraft carrier presence in the Gulf of Tonkin to five ships. General Westmoreland reported to the Joints Chief of Staff that the Việt Cộng were stronger than ever and that ARVN forces were taking heavy casualties and suffering from a high rate of desertions. Westmoreland said, "I see no course of action open to us except to reinforce our efforts in South Vietnam with additional U.S. or third country forces as rapidly as is practical." He identified specific U.S. units that would bring U.S. military strength in the country to forty-four combat battalions.

By the end of 1965, 1,928 Soldiers would be killed, and the number of troops serving in South Vietnam would grow to 184,300.

Spring could not come soon enough for Iggy; lacrosse was in season. Iggy had a lot of respect for Coach Adams and looked up to him not only as a coach but also as a mentor. "Ace" was his nickname and with good reason. He graduated from Johns Hopkins University in 1950. While he was there, JHU won the National Lacrosse Championship four times, 1947-1950. Coach Adams was a two-time first-team All-American pick at midfield, once in 1949 and again in 1950. He coached at Army for eleven years, and in his final year (1969), Army shared the USILA National Championship with Johns Hopkins. He went on to coach at the University of Pennsylvania and University of Virginia until he retired in 1992. He was the USILA Coach of the Year in 1961 and inducted into the National Lacrosse Hall of Fame in 1975.

Coaching lacrosse and winning was not his only interest; he, however, did achieve a coaching career record of 284 wins and 123 losses. He was also interested in developing young athletes into successful men as much as he was interested in teaching them the strategy of the game. Coach Adams said of intercollegiate athletics, "It sharpens your competitive nature, and that competitive spirit is important. The teamwork that you get at the college level is a very good learning experience. Being part of a team is doing something beyond yourself. It's part of the American way. Being a part of a team and working toward a goal is great training for young people to establish a work ethic."

Iggy played behind the cage again this year, and as was his style in high school, loved to move the ball around making plays, particularly when they were a man up. "He didn't have the speed as did some others on the team," said Coach Adams, "but he was persistent and determined in other ways."

Iggy loved to make plays and mix up his shots, sometimes on the ground and sometimes in the upper corners. His advice always stood out in my mind as I played the same position in high school. Ray always told me, "keep the goalie guessing; don't telegraph your shots."

Coach Adams explained Iggy's tenacity with loose balls: "We called him the 'Machine.' He was tremendous on loose balls, worked hard to get the ball off the ground. He was very willing to do anything for the team, wonderful spirit. He was completely unselfish. I don't think he had a selfish bone in his body."

Ed Sullivan also commented on Iggy's style of play. "When I think of him on the lacrosse field, I think of him as the consummate 'ground ball machine.' No matter the situation, either in a crowd trying to come up with the ball or just on his own, he was consistently the one who came up with the ball."

"He was all about the mission; mission to win or mission to succeed in the classroom or military training. He was a very persevering kind of guy. He wasn't apt to stray from what people of character would do. He was a role model in many ways, not just for me, but for [everyone] on the team," said Sullivan.

"Ray was so serious about whatever he did that was important to him—academics (with which he struggled), lacrosse, and the military," said teammate Glynn Hale. "Those of us in [Company] B-1 and on the lacrosse team never missed an opportunity to tease him about this seriousness because we admired his commitment but wanted to keep things light."

Glynn said, because of his short hair, "We would rub his head before a game for good luck. After a win, we would rub it again. I think he knew we were honoring him as much as teasing him."

The lacrosse season ended just prior to June Week 1966 with a record of 7-3, capped by a devastating loss to Navy, 7-16. Iggy had 12 goals and 13 assists for the season, second highest scorer next to Chris Pettit, who had 19 goals and 10 assists.

During the year, Ray strengthened his bond not only with teammates Chris Petit, Ed Sullivan, Larry Izzo, Glynn Hale, and others but also with his close friends Harry Rothmann and Mike Spinello. Those bonds were never broken.

Ray headed home for thirty days leave, then returned to West Point to greet the incoming class of Cadet Candidates. Assigned to the first detail of Beast Barracks for the next four weeks, Ray welcomed the opportunity to instill those disciplines in New Cadet Candidates that he once experienced and embraced.

His assignment complete, the first class trip was next. While one-half of his class comprised the second detail of Beast Barracks, for the next three weeks the other half participated in the Combat Arms Orientation Tour. Cadets visited Fort Benning, Georgia, for infantry orientation; Fort Sill, Oklahoma, for Artillery; Fort Knox, Kentucky for Armor; Fort Bliss, Texas, for Air Defense Artillery; and Fort Belvoir, Virginia, for Combat Engineers. Each of these stops would provide Ray insight into the latest technical and tactical developments of the U.S. Army's combat arms and serve as food for thought as to the branch of service he would eventually choose mid-way through Firstie year.

Chapter Seven

JUNE WEEK

"The lives and destines of valiant Americans
are entrusted to your care and leadership."

American Soldier's Memorial
West Point

A side from the black Athena class crest on their epaulets, you can always
spot a First Classman. They are confident, move with a swagger, and know
that in a little over 270 days, they will graduate from one of the finest educational and military leadership institutions in the world.

For Iggy and the Class of 1967, several positive and uplifting events occurred
during senior year. Under Coach Tom Cahill, the Army football team beat Navy
20-7 and finished the season with an outstanding record of 8-2. The taste of victory was sweet that year beating Kansas State 21-6, Penn State 11-0, Pittsburgh
28-0, and the University of California at Berkeley 6-3. Sports writers and fellow
coaches named Coach Cahill Coach of the Year.

Iggy and the Class of 1967 received their class rings in the fall of 1966, a
tradition that dates back to the Class of 1835. The Class Crest designed by a
committee of classmates symbolized the friendships developed over the four
years. On the other side of the ring was the Academy Crest consisting of the
Emblem of the Military Academy "borne on a shield and surmounted by a
crest" and the helmet of Pallas Athene positioned over a Greek sword and
fixed just below an eagle with the words Duty, Honor, Country embossed on
the fourteen carat gold scroll. Iggy wore his ring proudly with the Class Crest
facing inward.

Leadership development is an integral part of the West Point experience. Cadets study the techniques of historical leaders, and many opportunities are given

to take on that responsibility over the course of four years. For the first half of his First Class year, Iggy was on the First Regiment Staff as a Cadet Lieutenant and Assistant Regimental Adjutant. Selected to become Commander of Company B-1, this appointment continued to hone his leadership skills. As Company Commander, he was responsible for cadet discipline, morale, internal administration, and training for 135 cadets. This he enjoyed as he won the respect of those he commanded in the company.

On 4 June 1966, a three-page anti-war advertisement appeared in the *New York Times* signed by 6,400 teachers and professors. Anti-war sentiments existed, but failed to gain any traction.

General William Westmoreland requested more ground troops, and by year's end, ground forces in South Vietnam swelled to 385,000 troops. Seven divisions, including airborne, armored, army, and logistical units comprised American combat forces. As quickly as U.S. military units cleared the cities and hamlets of the Việt Cộng insurgents, they would return. The war of attrition was not changing the "political equation" in South Vietnam. Although the conflict realized significantly more insurgents killed during the year, 6,143 American troops would also fall by year-end.

It was February 1967. The Class of '67 filed into South Auditorium to choose their branch of service. This was a high-energy event where tradition reigned, branches chosen according to class rank. There were quotas for each branch, so as one became filled cadets chose another. If your father was a career officer in one of the other armed services - Air Force, Navy, or Marines - cadets had the option to join that arm of the U.S. military. Iggy impatiently waited to hear his name, *Raymond J. Enners.* He smartly shouted his choice of combat arms, *"Infantry!"* Larry Izzo chose Engineers. Chris Pettit chose Artillery. Glynn Hale, Harry Rothmann, Mike Spinello, and Ed Sullivan chose Infantry. A few months later, they would choose their first assignment. Iggy chose Fort Carson, Colorado.

Of the 583 cadets in the Class of 1967, 178 chose Artillery, and that was split between seven Air Defense Artillery and 171 Field Artillery; 169 chose Infantry; 79 chose Armor; 60 chose Corps of Engineers; and 55 chose Signal Corps. The remaining 42 fell into three categories: medically disqualified, foreign cadets, or those who chose other services.

As the depressing and dreary days of Gloom Period gave way to sunshine and shades of green throughout the Hudson Highlands, the excitement rose for the Firsties. Not only were they in the middle of their last semester of academics, they would shortly receive their new cars. Firsties ordered their cars during the fall of 1966, and now it was time to pick them up and take them for a spin. There were Shelby GTs, Mustangs, TR 6s, Corvettes, and other "hot" high horse-powered sets of wheels. Iggy chose a steel-blue Austin Healy, a fine British motor car, his pride and joy. It had plenty of spunk, was comfortable, and handled corners as if it was on rails.

Finding time to drive his car was a challenge as lacrosse was in season, his final year of intercollegiate athletics. Iggy played well in his final year, as did Army, losing only to Johns Hopkins, Maryland, and Navy. Losing to Navy was always a disappointment no matter what the sport. Iggy was in the hospital with mononucleosis just prior to the final game of the season with Navy at Annapolis.

Every member of the team was in suspense for days. Would Iggy play or would he sit out? Coach Adams and wife Betty drove Iggy to Annapolis. His memory about the incident was as vivid as if it happened yesterday. The doctor at West Point said, "Make sure the doctor at Annapolis checks him out before he plays." Coach Adams and Betty took him to the Navy hospital the day prior to the game. The doctor said he should stay in the hospital overnight for observation and recommended he not play. Thinking there was some ulterior motive, Adams was suspicious. "They said that it was for medical reasons. It bothered me at the time because Ray was so important to us on the extra man play." He was good at moving the ball and feeding the crease.

The symptoms he had did, in fact, indicate mononucleosis. The medical doctor at Annapolis was concerned that if hit hard enough, Iggy could suffer liver damage.

Obviously, Iggy was disappointed, as were his teammates. Mary Anne Pettit remembers the day before the Army-Navy game. "Ray had one more blood test to determine whether he would play in the game. The discussion with the doctor was the final word. [Ray suffered from an enlarged liver.] If he was hit, it could be quite dangerous."

Teammates rubbed Iggy's head and play began. Iggy stood on the sidelines in his lacrosse uniform and supported the team. He would not miss a game, even if he could not play. He was the spirit behind the team, on the field and off. In his eulogy of Iggy, Chris Pettit said of the Army team at halftime, "We'll never forget the vow made by an underdog Army team to win that game so that Iggy could step on the field and earn a [gold] star for beating Navy." Once again, tradition reigned. Players on any athletic team who beat Navy get a coveted gold star.

The fact that Iggy couldn't play "hurt us and we lost a close game 7-5 that year," said Adams. The season ended with 7 wins and 3 losses. Iggy had 16 goals and 7 assists. He won honorable mention All-American honors and was named to the North-South All-Star team. The coach's first team pick for the All-American team from Army included Chris on Attack and Glynn on Midfield.

June Week was approaching. On 6 June, the Class of '67 marched on to the parade grounds stepping lively to several tunes played by the Hell Cats. As the Firsties stood "front and center," the Hell Cats played the Alma Mater. The Corps "passed in review," a tradition for every graduating class whereby on the command *"eyes right,"* the parading cadet companies turn their heads and eyes slightly towards the graduating class as a gesture of respect.

The Hell Cats continued to play familiar army songs, including the prestigious *Official West Point March*, commonly known to the cadets as "Thumper." This inspirational tune embodies the essence of West Point, its ideals and traditions.

The Hell Cat's lineage dates back to the Revolutionary War when drummers and fifers were stationed on Constitution Island attached to Minutemen companies. They moved across the Hudson River when in 1778 General George Washington established the garrison at West Point.

June Week exemplified a new beginning for each class in the Corps. For the Plebes, it was "recognition day," recognition of withstanding the rigors and challenges of the first year and recognition of the responsibilities of being an upperclassman. For the Second and Third Classmen, it meant new leadership responsibilities. For Iggy and the other First Classmen, it meant pinning on the gold bars, committing to defend the Constitution of the United States, and leading Regular Army units around the world. In addition, for many in the Class of '67, including Iggy, it would mean defending the American ideals of freedom by leading combat units in the Republic of South Vietnam.

On the morning of the 7th, graduation day, a swearing-in ceremony conducted separately in each Cadet Company took place for the graduating Firsties. Once again, Iggy raised his right hand.

> I, Raymond James Enners, do solemnly swear that I will support
> and defend the Constitution of the United States against all enemies,
> foreign and domestic; that I will bear true faith and allegiance to the
> same; that I take this obligation freely, without any mental reserva-
> tion or purpose of evasion; and that I will and faithfully discharge the
> duties of the office upon which I am about to enter; so help me God.

Officially sworn-in, Iggy retreated to his barracks and prepared for the graduation ceremony at 10 a.m.; the day he was waiting for since R-Day, 1 July 1963.
It was a bright sunny day, and Michie Stadium, high above the Plain, was a fitting site for this prestigious and emotional event. The Academy grounds were
buzzing with activity. Family, relatives and friends lined the seats of the stadium.

The ceremony was inspirational in nature. General Ralph Edward Haines
Jr., Vice Chief of Staff of the Army, and General of the Army Omar Bradley
attended. Secretary of the Army Stanley R. Resor gave the graduation address.
He spoke of the qualities that West Point nurtured: integrity, idealism, consider-
ation for others, and a passion for service. He spoke of the patriotism of Soldiers
they would soon lead on the field of battle. And, he spoke of what makes the
military profession rewarding: "a sense of service to others and opportunity for
growth in knowledge, understanding, and responsibility." His comments were
encouraging and motivational.

One by one, the Class of '67 walked up to the platform to receive their diplomas, given according to the final order of merit, the highest member receiving
his first and so on throughout the class. As Iggy approached the rostrum, our
excitement soared. We were all proud of him and his accomplishments.

The last member of the class to receive his diploma carried the dubious dis-
tinction of being named the class "goat," a time honored tradition. He walked
proudly up the steps towards the podium, approached Secretary of the Army
Resor, left hand extended to receive his diploma, and saluted. He turned and
faced the class, diploma raised high above his head, pumped his arm in joyous
triumph, and smiled. The entire class gave him a standing ovation.

Closing remarks ended the ceremony. As Brigade Commander and Cadet
First Captain Jack Wood stood up and shouted *"Class Dismissed,"* the Class of
'67 in a euphoric gesture ceremoniously tossed their white caps towards the blue
sky. They were officially members of the Long Gray Line.

Immediately after the graduation exercises, Iggy reversed his class ring so that
the Academy Crest was closest to his heart–as did all cadets–a time honored
tradition that kept the Academy's Alma Mater and values Duty, Honor, Country

in one's mind at all times. The class ring represents a link between the graduate and the Long Gray Line, the succession of proud graduates dating back to 1802.

The ring also reflects with grandeur the importance of the West Point values. I remember reading General Douglas MacArthur's speech to the Corps of Cadets upon his receiving the Sylvanus Thayer Award in 1962. The title of the speech was "Duty, Honor, Country." Some might say these words are merely a slogan, but to a graduate of the Academy, they are a guiding light that one lives by. In MacArthur's words, they are a calling, they are values, they are a devotion to ideals.

> From the "poop deck" in the cadet mess hall MacArthur said:
> They are your rallying points to build courage when courage seems to fail, to regain faith when there seems to be little cause for faith, to create hope when hope becomes forlorn. They build your basic character. They mold you for your future roles as the custodians of the nation's defense. They make you strong enough to know when you are weak, and brave enough to face yourself when you are afraid. They teach you to be proud and unbending in honest failure, but humble and gentle in success; not to substitute words for actions, not to seek the path of comfort, but to face the stress and spur of difficulty and challenge.

These three words are what West Point instills in the Corps of Cadets. Some may fall short, but for most, these values assemble the forces of courage, responsibility, and pride when challenges seem insurmountable, when motives seem in conflict. Military tactics and strategies have changed over the years, but the meaning of West Point's values has not. The class ring is a constant reminder.

Of the 846 Cadet Candidates admitted on 1 July 1963, 583 graduated and incurred a four-year military obligation. They were uniquely patriotic as 545 served one or more tours in Vietnam. What would be their fate in light of the largest enemy offensive looming on the horizon, the *Tet* General Offensive and General Uprising? Few classes would experience the challenges and complexities of serving in the U.S. Army during these times.

Iggy was proud to be a West Pointer. He thought of West Point as a sacred place, a chronicle of military history where those that shaped the American past once walked. Humbled by their courage, by their duty, and by their sacrifice, he took it all in stride.

He was proud to embrace the ideals of Duty, Honor, Country–his heart of gray merely one product of West Point's rich vein of tradition. Just as R-Day was the beginning of his cadet career, graduation signified the beginning of his military career, a defining moment that would set him on a path of selfless service.

For those who are fortunate to experience its philosophy, teachings, and inspiration, the intangible magnetic like pull of West Point invades their very soul. A cadet may depart West Point on graduation day but usually returns, one way or another, in body or spirit. Mentally and emotionally, Iggy had a strong sense of devotion to the ideals of the Academy. After all, it had been his "rockbound highland home" for four years. He had a stronger understanding of integrity and loyalty that would carry him onward in his career, whatever and wherever that might be.

Iggy lived by the West Point ideals and principles that had guided many cadets throughout the history of the Academy. He had an increased understanding of himself, his capabilities, and future desires. Integrity to Ray meant taking responsibility for his actions, always seeking the "whole truth," thinking the best of others until proven otherwise, then assisting them to get on the right course. He was a team player–gave credit to others when success was achieved and "took the heat" when success seemed unattainable. He demonstrated moral courage in his dealings with others and physical courage in athletics.

This was Iggy's moral fiber. The choices he made in life revealed the true nature of his character. It was his strength, and when necessary, he dug deeper to do what was right.

After saying his goodbyes, he hopped into his Austin Healy and headed home. We followed. On the drive to Long Island, he keyed down and reflected on this unique four-year experience few have the opportunity to encounter.

The human hustle of cadets came to a grinding halt–silence over took the Academy. The newly commissioned lieutenants were off on a sixty day leave; all other classes took thirty. In the absence of the cadets, for the next thirty days, the austere patriotic poses of Washington, Kosciuszko, Patton, Sedgwick, and Thayer would watch over the Academy grounds.

On 3 July, a new class of Cadet Candidates would arrive, of which I was one, the Class of 1971; "Professionally Done in '71"–my four years at the Academy beginning, Iggy's ending.

Shortly, Iggy would be off on a new mission, a mission that would further test his mental and physical strength. He enjoyed new challenges. This one would further increase his self-confidence and elevate his skills.

Chapter Eight

HARMONY CHURCH

"No human being knows how sweet sleep is
but a soldier."

Colonel John S. Mosby
(USA Ret.)

With the warm summer air swiftly flowing over the windshield of his new Austin Healey, Ray approached the front gate at Fort Benning in Columbus, Georgia at 6:00 p.m. It was 5 August. Fully rested after sixty days leave, he was ready to take on the next challenge, the Infantry Officers Basic Course (IOBC) and then Ranger School. IOBC Class #2 began on 7 August. Because Ray would be attending Ranger School, the basic training course was an abbreviated version of the course typically given to other second lieutenants assigned to the infantry combat arms. It was a refresher course of what he learned during the summer training sessions at West Point, beginning with Camp Buckner, except it focused almost entirely on infantry weapons and tactics.

"The training down here is pretty good but we've had a lot of it before," Ray wrote in the letter to my parents on 23 August. "The hours are very long and we have very little free time. Two or three days a week we don't finish work until 12:30 in the morning and we get up for PT [physical training] at 5:15 every morning."

IOBC lasted thirty-six days. Two hundred nine officers graduated on 12 September 1967.

Protests against the war in Vietnam picked up momentum. Earlier in the year, anti-war activists seized five buildings at New York's Columbia University. Protests were a mix of political views and brainstorming ideas. Activities varied; demonstrations, congressional lobbying, "teach-ins," civil disobedience, and draft resistance fueled the unrest. Three hundred thousand protestors demonstrated in the streets of New York. In October, 50,000 anti-war activists surrounded the Pentagon, resulting in 700 arrests. Some called it social ignorance. Others called it free speech or social unrest against the policies of the mainstream. It did eventually sway government policy.

Congressional lobbying became more prevalent, and although in 1965 the general population supported the war, by this time only thirty-five percent felt America's objective and strategies in Vietnam were appropriate. Support for the war steadily eroded, and accusations from pacifists and some politicians surfaced that the level of destruction that war imposed was immoral. The media rapidly turned negative. General Westmoreland argued that the media played a significant role in turning the public against the war.

Also at this time, the Communist Politburo in Hanoi began planning a major military offensive known as *Tet*, a highly integrated military and political assault on South Vietnam that would surely defeat the U.S. and its Allies. General Võ Nguyên Giáp made two assumptions about the American forces: one, the U.S troop strength would not increase over the current levels of about 400,000, and two, the anti-war sentiments in the U.S., particularly in an election year, would cause President Johnson to capitulate. General Giáp also made two assumptions about the South Vietnamese Army: one, the ARVN would put up little resistance and might even collapse, and two, after the communist victory, the South Vietnamese populace would rise up against and overthrow the Saigon regime. Neither of the assumptions by Giáp turned out to be true.

In September 1967, North Vietnam tested America's reactions by shelling U.S. bases along Route 9 south of the Demilitarized Zone (DMZ) in the Central Highlands. The NVA hit Khe Sanh, a marine outpost at the western end of Route 9. They struck Special Forces bases at Loc Ninh and Dak To in Kontum Province. The U.S. and ARVN committed sixteen battalions to these areas to fend off the enemy. The attacks were diversionary tactics in the rural areas designed to draw U.S. forces away from the population centers. While the North Vietnamese Army attacked in the rural areas, the Việt Cộng infiltrated the population centers. During the artillery shelling of these combat bases, for the most part, the U.S forces remained on the "tactical defensive."

Ranger School

Ray reported to Harmony Church for Ranger School immediately after the basic training course. Assigned to Class #4 along with several of his West Point classmates, the many faces of Fort Benning would be his home for the next two months. Beginning June 1967 Ranger School was mandatory for all newly commissioned Regular Army Officers. It remained that way until June 1971 when General Westmoreland directed that it become voluntary. Ranger training was a means to an end. At that time, the majority of each class would serve in Vietnam. Unlike in peacetime when Soldiers train and then train some more, this training had a specific purpose. Ray would experience squad and platoon level tactics, ambushes, raids, navigation, extended patrolling, reconnaissance, and survival training in three very different geographical environments, all to prepare him for the rigors of combat.

Rangers "Lead the Way" was a fitting motto for officers and NCOs about to see combat, but it did not at all describe the punishing training Ray experienced.

What was Ranger School like, you ask? "It was miserable beyond all imagination. It's an incredibly grueling and difficult experience both physically and mentally," said Freed Lowrey, Ray's classmate.

Freed Lowrey retired as a Lieutenant Colonel and served two tours in Vietnam, his first tour cut short after he received wounds as a rifle platoon leader with Bravo Company 3-503rd, 173rd Airborne Brigade. He also served as a Recon Platoon Leader and Assistant Brigade S3 (operations). During his second tour, he commanded a rifle company in the 1-52nd, 198th Brigade, Americal Division. He was wounded once again after seven and a half months, which ended his tour of duty. During his service in Vietnam, Freed earned three Bronze Star Medals with Valor, three Bronze Star Medals for meritorious service, four Purple Hearts, The Vietnamese Cross of Gallantry with Gold Star, an Air Medal, and the CIB.

"It's a very physical experience. As hard as it was, it was the best training I could have had to prepare me for Vietnam," said Ed Sullivan.

Harry Rothmann added, "Ranger training was the best training the U.S. Army had at the time before going into combat. It places you in sustained combat type conditions, not that somebody is shooting back at you. It's the strain of the deprivation of sleep, hardships, marching tens of miles, fifty to sixty miles in two days that brings out the combat character in you."

Harry reflected on his combat assignment in Vietnam and emphasized the benefit of his experience at Ranger School. He went on to say," When I was in Vietnam, I was under similar conditions, and I was able to get through all of it."

Ranger School tested the limits of personal fatigue and endurance. It also taught infantry officers and NCOs good judgment–to be aggressive in pursuit of the mission, to take the initiative–and not make decisions based on personal wellbeing.

"A lack of toughness or not being demanding causes leaders to make decisions based on their personal comfort and needs rather than what is needed to win and keep soldiers alive," said Glynn Hale. He recalled a case in point where the lack of judgment and aggressiveness cost lives. The mission involved a routine company size combat assault into a "one-ship" LZ in the I Corps Tactical Zone near the DMZ.

> Each Chalk unloaded and stood around before moving into position on the expanding perimeter. Despite pleas from the aircraft flight leader to clear the LZ more quickly, nothing changed. The sixth aircraft landed, unloaded, took off, [its] skid hit a stump and crashed on the LZ–the rotor blades killing eight soldiers who had not moved immediately to their position on the perimeter.

A fitting example where being aggressive by setting expectations for a mission, proper training, and enforcing standard operating procedures would have saved lives. The commanding officer was complacent and sloppy.

Glynn's unscientific observation of rifle companies in Vietnam concluded that aggressive commanders in combat suffered fewer casualties and inflicted more enemy casualties than less aggressive commanders. He also indicated that "passive" commanders suffered more non-combat related incidences.

The history of the coveted "Black and Gold" Ranger Tab dates back to the Korean War, 3 November 1950, when the first tabs were awarded to the 1st, 2nd, 3rd, and 4th Airborne Ranger Infantry Companies. Over the years, controversy arose as to the criteria for the award. Should Soldiers serving in Ranger units be permitted to wear the tab as some did in World War II, or should it be reserved for those that complete the arduous Ranger Course? Since 1961, the criteria remained unchanged; only those who successfully complete the Ranger Course can wear the coveted Black and Gold.

The Ranger Tab "is a symbol of those who have explored the outer limits of the human spirit. It is a statement of the volunteer Brotherhood, who choose to

EARLY YEARS

Ray, pictured far right, with his brother Rich and sister Sandra.

Ray's catch after an early morning fishing expedition on Lake Winnipesauke.

High School

Ray Enners — Mr. Machine. This illustration was posted on Ray's high school locker.

Ray Enners, Senior Class President, Half Hollow Hills, 1963.

The Half Hollow Hills High School football team, ca. 1962.

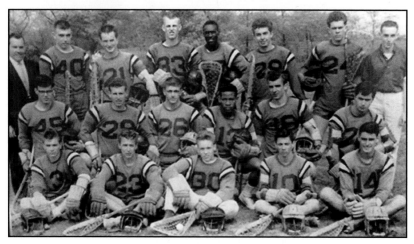

The Half Hollow Hills High School lacrosse team, ca. 1963.

Close up of Ray, number 26.

Ray, pictured here in football gear, was captain of the football and lacrosse teams. Pictured also is coach Bill Martens, Jim Sharback and assistant coach Robert Domozych.

4th Year - Plebe

Ray at Reception Day, West Point, 1 July 1963.

Cadet candidates on the march, to trophy point for the swearing in ceremony, 1 July 1963. Ray is pictured in the far left row, first in line toward the camera.

Reception Day at West Point, 1 July 1963. Pictured l-r: Mom, Ray, Dad.

Plebe year, 1964, Princeton vs. Army. Pictured l-r: Ray, Chris Pettit, and Warren Dempsy.

3RD YEAR - YEARLING

Yearling year, Ray with parents, 19 September 1964.

No. 26 Ray Enners scores against Syracuse, 3rd classman. Courtesy of Slum and Gravy, USMA, 27 May 1965.

2ND YEAR - COW

2nd classman, West Point, September 1965.

Army vs. Rutgers, Warren Dempsey (14) scores and Ray (26) gets the assist, 9 April 1966.

1st Year - Firstie

Cadet Raymond J. Enners. Courtesy of Howitger Studios, West Point, New York

First Regiment staff, 1966. Cadet Captain L.L. Izzo is standing first row, second from left; Cadet Captain G.W. Hale is standing first row, far right; and Ray is standing second row, far left.

Raymond J. Enners, Cadet Captain, Co. B-1, West Point, October 1966.

Pictured l-r: Ed Sullivan, Chris Pettit, Ray, and Larry Izzo, Spring 1967.

Army vs. Yale, 1 April 1967. Ray is pictured in the foreground beside the net.

Raymond J. Enners in full dress gray, 1967. Courtesy of Howitzer Studios, West Point, New York.

Graduation Day, West Point, 7 June 1967.

Ray stands with his mother and sister after graduating from West Point.

In his 1st class year (Firstie), Ray was featured on the cover of International Lacrosse Magazine, Summer 1967.

Pre-Vietnam

Ray loads up his car before heading to Fort Carson, Colorado, his first duty assignment while his father lends a hand.

Ray coached lacrosse at the Air Force Academy while stationed at Fort Carson, Colorado, here seen with the Plebe Lacrosse Team, Spring 1968.

Vietnam

2000 lb. bomb craters in the Song Tra Khuc Valley. Courtesy of John McNown.

Al Matheson Battle of Nui Hoac Ridge prior to airlift to LZ Ross 18 May 1968 Courtesy of Al Matheson.

Alpha Company on patrol. Courtesy of Bill Adams.

Cpt. William Adams, SFC William Wright, and LTC William D. Guinn Courtesy of Bill Adams.

Ha Thanh Special Forces Camp, 1968. Courtesy of Michael Fairlie.

Lt. Michael Mooney, SP4 Bob Sheen (RTO), and SP5 David Doc Bushey Courtesy of Ken Melesky.

LZ Bronco. Courtesy of Larry Holiday.

LZ Liz. Courtesy of Frank Schurich.

LZ Liz-Lt. John McNown, PFC Nick Polizzi-RTO, Sgt. Randy Less, SP4 Joe Novotny, SP4 Val Longmore, and SP4 Bob Sheen-RTO at LZ Liz. Courtesy of John McNown.

LZ Thunder, 1968. Courtesy of John McNown.

OP7 Ha Thanh Special Forces Camp, 1968. Courtesy of John McNown.

Sgt. Kermit Williams, Danny Thomas, Sgt. Ronald Biggs, SP4 Eugene Stevens, and Sgt. Michael Sheppard. Courtesy of Tommy Acosta.

Song Tra Khuc Valley near Ha Thanh. Courtesy of John McNown.

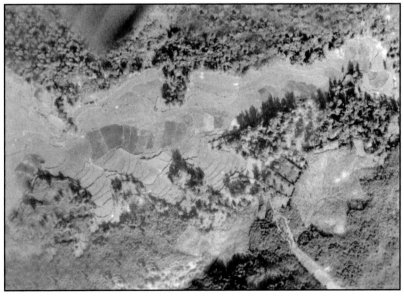

Site of Hedgerow Action 18 September 1968. Courtesy of John McNown

SP4 Ray DeVincent (left forefront) and Cpt. William Adams (partially hidden) capture of one of two suspected VC following the Battle of Nui Hoac Ridge, May 1968. Courtesy of Al Matheson.

Post Vietnam

*Actual plate for the first Lt. Raymond J. Enners Award for the
Outstanding Collegiate Lacrosse Player in the Nation.*

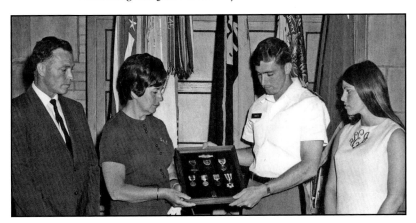

*Presentation of a posthumous award to the parents of 1st Lt. Raymond J. Enners. Pictured l-r:
Mr. and Mrs. Raymond H. Enners, Cadet Richard Enners (Class of '71), and Miss Sandra J.
Enners. Courtesy USMA.*

Foley, Enners, Nathe Lacrosse Center, designed by Baker Barrios Architects for the West Point Association of Graduates, opening Spring 2017, lead donor - William P. Foley II.

Half Hollow Hills Vietnam Memorial. Courtesy of Gary and Linda Foster.

Larry and Terri Izzo at the dedication ceremony for the Kimsey Athletic Center, West Point, August 2003. Courtesy of Ed and Mary Sullivan.

Mrs. Gloria Enners and Ed Sullivan at the dedication ceremony for the Kimsey Athletic Center, West Point, August 2003. Courtesy of Ed and Mary Sullivan.

Mrs. Gloria Enners and Mary Sullivan at the dedication ceremony for the Kimsey Athletic Center, West Point, August 2003. Courtesy of Ed and Mary Sullivan.

Ed Sullivan, Ray Bigelman, and Rich Enners (presenter) at the West Point Inspiration to Serve Cemetery Tour, Class of 2017, April 2015.

Cadre handed out operations orders for patrols late in the evening, and preparation was required. Typically candidates were in bed at 2400 hours and up at 0330 hours. On occasion, Lane Graders would detonate artillery simulators in the early morning hours. Peaceful sleep, don't count on it; you had to be alert, always. Sometimes there was no time for breakfast; you were always on the go.

"Ranger School taught you how to listen", recalls Freed. "It gave you self-confidence. It taught you how to adapt and be flexible."

Heat and humidity did not cause any discomfort during this phase as it was the fall of the year; however, Ray and his Ranger Buddy Ed would soon find out that the cold temperatures of the Georgia Mountains would test their resolve.

Mountain Phase

Welcome to Camp Merrill high in the Chattahoochee National Forest just outside of Dahlonega, Georgia. After a six hour ride from Fort Benning in a "duce-and-a-half", the military version of a transport truck, Ray and Ranger Buddy Ed arrived at Camp Merrill. Not exactly a luxury vehicle, it had a stiff suspension, wooden seats, and growled like an angry lion.

This phase included mountaineering, repelling (day and night), night tactical missions, and patrolling, all designed to strengthen skills, build confidence, and prepare each officer for the mountainous terrain of Vietnam.

Ray tied knots typically used in mountaineering exercises. He repelled with and without his sixty-five pound rucksack, and "buddy" repelled with a man strapped to his back, simulating the transport of an injured comrade.

They conducted raids, ambushes, air assaults, and extended patrols. The environment was more severe than the Benning Phase for two reasons. First, it was cold. Ed Sullivan said, "Enduring the cold was another part of getting prepared." Second, the mountains were steep with ridgelines, inclines, downed trees, and exposed rocks.

Ed recalled one operation where he and Ray had to make an Australian raft. They stripped down to shorts and shirt, created a raft with their poncho and other gear, and had to ford a stream. "It got down to the 30s the night before, and of course we did it in the early morning. We were shivering," said Ed. During that time of year, the water levels were low in the mountain streams. The Lane Grader found a pool of water just to make it more miserable. "We grit our teeth and just did it," said Ed. When Ed finished Ranger School, he said to Mary, his wife, "I don't ever want to get out of bed and put my feet on bare concrete."

Ranger candidates lived in wooden Hooches that held eight men. Ray said, "If you've seen the movie *The Dirty Dozen*, [Hooches] are exactly like the huts the convicts lived in. This is an improvement over Camp Darby at Benning where we slept outside in sleeping bags."

Patrolling during the Mountain Phase consumed a large part of the course, as it simulated what platoon leaders would experience in Vietnam. There were hardships and challenges like ravines, marshes, and cliffs, and one comical event in particular.

While on a day patrol near a cattle farm, Ray and Ed decided to cut through a fenced-in pasture. They had walked about half way across the pasture when a bull came out of nowhere charging at full speed. The faster they ran, the faster it galloped after them. Fortunately, they hopped the fence before the bull got too close. Ed said, "It was clearly one of the more frightening things, but afterwards one of the funniest things that ever happened to us."

"We have mountaineering training tomorrow and the next day we will depart on an extended three-day patrol," said Ray. Through the streams and underbrush carrying a sixty-five pound "ruck", small arms ammunition, and sometimes an M60 machine gun, Ray and Ed humped; wet, tired, and hungry. They ate once every twenty-four hours on this particular extended patrol. The cadre graded patrol leaders in this phase on their ability to tie knots and repel.

Ray lived strictly under combat conditions just as if he were on a Search and Clear operation in enemy territory. He ate C-Rations while on patrol and a small portion of rice just as the Vietnamese and Việt Cộng did since it was lightweight but filling. "You wouldn't believe the things you carry while on patrol, said Ray. You have things taped to you, every pocket is full, plus ammo, signal flares, and smoke grenades.

"I was patrol leader for part of the patrol and got a satisfactory grade. All I need is two more satisfactory grades and I will pass the course.

"The other night I was on point, 1st man in the file, and I actually had to cut my way through the biggest briar patch I've ever seen with my knife. Everyone walks around like a zombie with red eyes 'cause we get very little sleep," said Ray.

"The main thing is we are learning a lot.

"The weather is amazing. It's about 70 degrees during the day and about 40-50 degrees during the night. Since we operate mostly at night we usually freeze."

Ranger school tested Ray's ability to listen and adapt. Freed remembered on one patrol, "Right in the middle of the patrol the Lane Grader killed the patrol leader [figuratively] and turned to me and said, 'You are the new patrol leader.' You always had to know what the mission was and the situation."

Ray said, "We've almost forgotten what it's like to live like a civilian. Here, you're dirty all of the time so you hardly ever think about taking a shower; they're few and far between. The man who forgets his toilet paper from the C-Rations [box] is just plain out of luck."

"We get a lot of laughs though. Some pretty funny things happen when you're out walking through some of the dense terrain and vegetation and you can't even see your hand when you hold it in front of you. When you hear someone splashing around and a loud *Damn* breaks the silence of the night, you know someone has just fallen chest deep into a stream."

Ray's time in the mountains ended. Tired and hungry, he returned to Camp Merrill. He and Ed traveled in military trucks back to Fort Benning, where they would take a shower or two, or maybe three, and eat a decent meal. There were two breaks for the ranger candidates, one each between phases, all of six hours. He ate and slept.

One more phase to go, in the Florida swamps, just outside of Elgin Air Force Base.

★ ★ ★

Florida Phase

This was perhaps the most challenging phase in terms of mental and physical stress. Harry recalled, "Our missions in Florida were geared to prepare us directly for infantry operations in Vietnam. We raided base camps. We did search and destroy missions." From Camp Rudder, Ranger Candidates conducted all long-range patrols through the Florida jungle, swamps, and marshes. It was home to Florida's finest reptiles, water moccasins and alligators. Ambushes, reconnaissance missions, and stream crossings rounded out a Ranger's knowledge of small unit tactics that would dominate a leader's challenges in Vietnam.

Ray and Ed prepared themselves mentally for this punishing final phase, particularly patrolling. Ed recalled, "We would patrol with one ration a day." How long they would be in the swamps was always an agonizing question. On one particular patrol, it was for ten days. "You learned mental toughness," said Ed. "Patrolling became second nature to you." Tactical competence was important as NCOs and enlisted personnel catch on very quickly if a leader lacks the required tactical skills. They lose confidence and perform at substandard levels. On some patrols, they moved all night without sleep.

Freed remembered one patrol during this phase that taught him a lesson he never forgot. It was a night patrol maybe 1,700 or 1,800 meters. Freed was the compass man. It was dark, pitch black dark, almost like being blind. The terrain was rolling hills, and they had to cross two streams. There were two azimuth changes during the extent of the patrol, and Freed arrived at the objective within ten meters of dead center. "I learned to trust my compass, believe in my compass, because sometimes you will think to yourself, this doesn't feel right," said Freed. This turned out to be wise advice, particularly on three and a half hours of sleep.

Humping through the swamps with little sleep and dining on C-Rations pushed the limits of human capabilities. "Trench foot" was a problem for some; better carry enough powder and dry socks and change them frequently. As JD Lock put it, by this stage of the course, everyone was in a "catatonic, drone state of mind." Conditions were brutal–the body exhausted, muscles screaming and lungs burning–but you could not give in. Rangers had to be fully conscious of the mission and the health and safety of the men in their unit. Rangers focused on the mission, the task at hand, not the discomforts.

The last part of the Florida Phase was a night patrol and an attack on a simulated objective. The Lane Grader told Ed's patrol, if they find food on the objective, *do not* touch it. As they approached the objective, they spotted cases of C-Rations piled up in a scattered manner. In a frenzy, some tore apart the cases to get at the food. The Lane Graders knew that would happen. Little did the candidates know there was a penalty for not following instructions, an eighteen mile forced march back to Camp Rudder. The Lane Grader that led the march reminded Ed of "Mr. Clean" who appeared in TV commercials for cleaning solutions, a tall, bald, long-legged, muscle-bound man wearing a white T-shirt. "He took one stride, and everyone had to take three just to catch up," said Ed. Guys were falling over and falling out. "I did OK," said Ed. "I was in good shape from running." He trotted back; it was easier for him.

With the completion of the march back to base camp, the third phase ended. Ray and his comrades traveled back to Fort Benning by bus for the much anticipated graduation ceremony. Graduation ended and the coveted Black and Gold Tab was pinned to the upper sleeve of the left arm. Of the 283 Ranger candidates that began the course, 223 graduated.

Ranger School embodies the "know" of the U.S. Army's leadership model. Ray knew that graduating from the highly acclaimed training course he would be stronger mentally and physically and better prepared to take on what would lie ahead. He now had the small unit tactical skills he would depend on when leading his infantry platoon in Vietnam. Having experienced a combat tour, Harry Rothmann said:

Knowing the tactics, techniques, and weaponry of small infantry units is also critical and must be mastered. You have to be the master infantryman in the platoon. At the company level, too, particularly because Vietnam operations were conducted at the small unit level. Competency is two-fold: you must know tactics, techniques, and weaponry, and you have to be able to apply it. The only way to apply it is to know your leaders in the unit and gain their trust.

Ray and Ed departed for my aunt and uncle's apartment on Peachtree Street in Atlanta. "The ride to Atlanta was horrendous," recalled Ed. Ray's Austin Healy had a lot of spunk, and Ed was driving a Pontiac Grand Prix. He could not keep up with Ray or stay awake. "I had the windows open and the radio blaring, trying to stay awake," said Ed. Ed finally caught up to Ray and waved him over and said, "I have to get coffee or cokes."

They finally arrived in Atlanta. As they approached the front door, Ray noticed a welcome note from my aunt taped to it. Their eyes widened with joy as the note said there were two steaks in the refrigerator. Rangers are always tired and hungry, either during the course or immediately after.

They couldn't take enough showers. While one took a shower, the other cooked the steaks. They ate the steaks, and then one cleaned up while the other took a shower. Ed recalled, "I remember Johnny Carson coming on the television, and Ed McMahon saying, '*Here's Johnny!*'" Ed was out. That's all he remembered until the next morning.

Following a long night's sleep, they traveled to Baltimore and went directly to Mary's house. After greeting them, she remarked that they both needed showers. Ray rested for the night and drove home to Farmingdale the next morning. He returned to Baltimore to take part in Ed's wedding on 19 November.

Ray arrived in Baltimore two days before the wedding, and that evening Ray, Ed, and Mary went to an upscale restaurant, the Greenspring Inn. Mary set Ray up with a blind date, one of her friends. Having just finished Ranger School about a week before, they were constantly hungry. They sat down to eat. By the time Ray finished his dinner, he noticed that his date was dabbling with her food. Ray looked at her and pointed to a baked potato on her plate and asked, "Are you going to eat that?" She said, "Probably not." Ed said, "Ray speared it, put it on his plate, and finished that off, too."

U.S. Army

Ray finished his formal training and moved on to his first assignment at Fort Carson, Colorado in early December. There he would be a platoon leader in Charlie Company, 1st Battalion 61st Infantry Regiment, 5th Infantry Division. The Army required that all officers have a stateside Regular Army unit assignment before a combat tour in Vietnam. He spent a great deal of time in the field on maneuvers and loved the practical application of what he had learned in Ranger School.

Having spent five years in the Army, I had some knowledge of the U.S. Army's culture and values. It is the best leadership institution in the world. They promote from within, unlike corporations do, for obvious reasons. Consequently, they have the best training to move officers and NCOs up in rank and responsibility. Their leadership model, "Be, Know, Do," is known throughout the world. Combine "Be," a Soldier's core values; with "Know," competence and wisdom; and "Do," taking appropriate action depending on the situation. This model far surpasses any dictionary definition of leadership. Their ethos embodies all that a leader should be, can be, and must be to achieve results without exposing Soldiers to undue risk.

Tet Offensive

It was January 1968. Ray was back at Fort Carson, and I had returned to West Point to begin my second semester of Plebe year, when we heard the news about *Tet*. It blanketed every news station. The objective of *Tet* was to strike a major blow against the Allied forces in the major populated areas as well as cause the South Vietnamese populace to rise up against the central government in Saigon and the city and district governments throughout the south. The Communists intended to destroy America's confidence that a war of attrition could not be won.

The *Tet* lunar New Year begins on the first day of the first month of the Vietnamese calendar, typically late January or early February. Since the beginning of the conflict, there was a thirty-six hour cease-fire respected by all, and this year it would go into effect at 1800 hours on 29 January. Different from previous years, communist forces massed on the border of Laos and Cambodia. They were planning to strike in the early morning hours of 30 January, which was a surprise to U.S. and ARVN forces.

ARVN Intelligence and Headquarters Military Assistance Command Vietnam (MACV) received a series of reports that a large-scale attack would occur three months prior but thought it was just propaganda. Through their network of agents, ARVN Intelligence discovered a Resolution 13 released from the North Vietnamese Politburo that called for "victory in a short time and prescribed the strategy of large-scale offensive to achieve it."

Another document dated 1 September 1967 and intercepted on 25 October highlighted a two part objective for the communist forces: one, the end of American presence in South Vietnam, and two, a three-prong offensive designed to defeat the Republic of Vietnam Armed Forces (RVNAF), destroy U.S. political and military institutions, and instigate a country-wide insurrection of the popular masses.

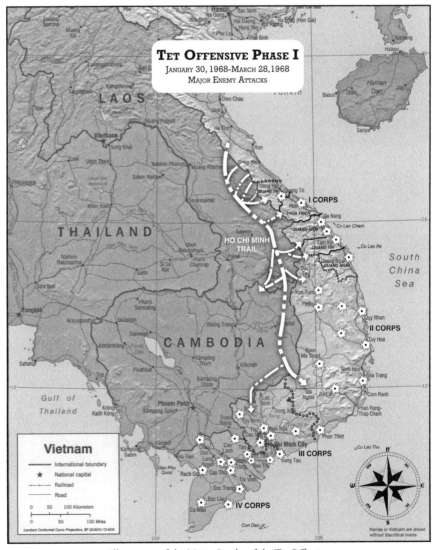

Illustration of the Major Battles of the Tet Offensive

The signs of a massive offensive by the communists were there, but due to a lack of focus on the intention of the communists and lack of coordination among agencies of the ARVN Joint General Staff (JCS), ARVN Intelligence, and MACV, the situation was completely misread. There was also a lack of information sharing between the high levels of both ARVN JCS and MACV.

So it began, 30 January 1968. Communist forces attacked and fired upon thirty-six of forty-four provincial capitals, sixty-four of 242 district capitals, and some fifty hamlets. They also attacked air bases. The most noted attacks by the communists were in Saigon, the ancient city of Hue, and the mountain resort of Dalat, a center of both leisure and power. Fierce fighting ensued, but the Allied forces repelled the attacks. It was a major "tactical defeat" for both the Việt Cộng and North Vietnamese Army and a major "tactical victory" for the Allies.

The U.S. strategy of adapting, flexible thinking, and maneuvering proved successful. General Westmoreland strengthened the support around the major cities by massing several battalions of Soldiers, which proved to be a significant factor in the Allies defeating the communists. The Allies used their firepower and weaponry effectively and maneuvered their forces quickly and efficiently.

Tet took a significant toll on the communist forces. Their strength waned in the face of superior allied firepower and maneuverability. They lost approximately 30,000 to 45,000 troops during the first ten days of the *Tet* Offensive.

On the other hand, the first *Tet* Offensive was a strategic win for North Vietnam. It began to galvanize the American public at home *against* the war. Antiwar sentiments accelerated, and the public became more fixated on the military strategy as an instrument of U.S. government policy. Peace movements and civil disobedience became more common. I remember as a Yearling at West Point, students from a nearby college wearing black armbands would demonstrate outside Thayer Gate, the main entrance to the Academy. Demonstrations were uneventful compared to the more populated cities where protestors thought they could rally more sympathizers.

News media bias became more prevalent. They sensationalized the government's military strategies, its policies and combat operations in Vietnam. Antiwar sentiment spilled over into various aspects of American culture. "Teach-ins" became more widespread. They attracted people from labor, business, and different religions. Tactics included debates, petitions, and lobbying. Burning draft cards followed.

Walter Cronkite, CBS News anchor, commented at the end of his February 27, 1968, broadcast.

Who won and who lost in the great Tet offensive against the cities? I'm not sure. The Vietcong did not win by a knockout, but neither did we. The referees of history may make it a draw. It seems now more certain than ever that the bloody experience of Vietnam is to end in a stalemate. But it is increasingly clear to this reporter that the only rational way out then will be to negotiate, not as victors, but as honorable people who lived up to their pledge to defend democracy, and did the best they could.

Horror, jubilation, and discontent infiltrated the spring and summer of 1968. On 4 April, James Earl Ray assassinated Dr. Martin Luther King, and on 6 June Bobby Kennedy suffered a similar fate at the hands of twenty-two year old Palestinian Sirhan Sirhan.

While Ray was at Fort Carson, there was reason to celebrate as James Keating, lacrosse Coach of United States Air Force Academy in Colorado Springs, asked Ray if he would like to help coach the Plebe team. Ray's love of the game caused him not to think twice. Throughout the season, he helped the inexperienced players with stick skills, dodging, and strategy. Ray's passion for the game shined through and made a lasting impression on the coaches and players alike. Plebe Coach Major Bill Francke remembered the pre-game pep talk prior to the Rutgers game. "Ray gave them some sincere words of wisdom about being a real winner and how the little guy can beat the big guy if he has the desire and the heart," said Bill. The underdog Air Force Plebes beat Rutgers in a close game.

On 7 June, Ray's promotion to First Lieutenant added some excitement, a welcomed change to the "butter-bar" ridicule that comes with wearing the gold second lieutenant's insignia.

August gave way to more anti-war demonstrations. At the Democratic National Convention in Chicago, tens of thousands of protestors battled police in the streets. Demonstrators confronted 12,000 local police, 7,500 Illinois National Guardsmen, 7,500 Army Soldiers, and 1,000 Secret Service Agents. All of America witnessed the protests on television. There were accusations of police brutality, and eventually trials ensued. America was in turmoil not only due to anti-war sentiments; racial tensions escalated soon after the slaying of Dr. King.

Confusion blanketed the United States. The American people began to turn against the fighting Soldiers and the war rapidly. Vietnam was a unique war, a war of insurgency, a war of attrition where "body counts" was the primary measure of progress, not the accumulation of turf. There were no "fronts" as there were in World War I and II—and little alignment between U.S. Government policy towards the war and military strategy. The objectives of the war were unclear. America was fighting a war on foreign soil without the support of the American people, and that would prove to be disastrous in the coming years. The pressures of the war on Soldiers were immense, yet America's military leaders and youth performed admirably.

Chapter Nine

CHAMPAIGN GROVE

"I will always do my duty, no matter what the price.
I've counted up the cost, I know the sacrifice.
Oh, and I don't want to die for you,
But if dying's asked of me,
I'll bear that cross with honor,
'Cause freedom don't come free."

Toby Keith, *American Soldier*

I t was September now, and the monsoon rains were heavy, making movement in the bush complicated and infinitely more unbearable.

Phase III of *Tet* was in full swing. The offensive began on 17 August with rocket and mortar attacks on Đà Nẵng and Tây Ninh. "Attacks by Fire" in the four Tactical Zones was the primary approach used by the VC and NVA. By design, Attacks by Fire delivered the enemy payload from a distance. It allowed them to quickly scatter and limit their exposure to friendly return fire from artillery, Tac Air and gunships. Phase III was the weakest of the three phases with only fifteen major attacks across South Vietnam compared to fifty-two in Phase II. Of these fifteen, only two were of battalion size or larger.

Hanoi did not align offensive attacks with propaganda programs during this phase, as the NVA learned from previous initiatives that inciting a rebellion with the South Vietnamese populace was not going to win them over. Nor did the Việt Cộng or NVA attack Saigon with main forces; they used local poorly trained insurgents sympathetic to the cause. Because of the severe losses suffered during the first two phases of *Tet,* some communist military units deactivated and reassigned troops to other units. Many of Việt Cộng planned attacks failed to draw Allied troops away from the major cities, a serious miscalculation on the part of North Vietnam military leaders. From a tactical standpoint, the effects of the Allied initiatives seriously hindered the fighting capability of the VC and NVA during the third phase, the Allied forces repelling the advances of the North Vietnamese Army and Việt Cộng throughout the four Tactical Zones.

A document captured by the South Vietnamese Army during the final phase of *Tet* II indicated the NVA high command issued a standing order to attack and withdraw–and not become involved in sustained combat with Allied forces. The order also stipulated that the enemy was to draw Allied forces away from the cities by striking in the rural areas. A diary captured by ARVN during the early stages of Phase III indicated, "Everybody [North Vietnamese Army and Việt Cộng] is tired and confused. Many don't want the unit to break down into small elements because it would be easily destroyed by enemy [U.S. and ARVN] attacks. The enemy [U.S. and ARVN forces] is more active, more numerous, and enjoys the initiative."

Operation Champaign Grove

The Allies launched additional combat initiatives in the fall and early winter months throughout the four Tactical Zones. One such offensive in the I Corps area was Operation Champaign Grove that took place in Quảng Ngãi Province, beginning 4 September, and involved Alpha Company and Ray's platoon. It was this military offensive that further tested Ray's character and leadership, as he led his platoon in two harrowing firefights.

"We're expecting a big attack in a short while to come in this area," said Ray. "The VC and NVA are starting to mass in the mountains just west of here." Communist troops would use the Hồ Chí Minh Trail to launch their attacks, re-supply operating units in the rural areas and cities, and when necessary, retreat to this safe haven. Allied forces in the I Corps Tactical Zone prevented further attacks on the population centers by sealing off vital North Vietnamese supply routes from Laos through the A Shau Valley.

Lieutenant Colonel Guinn echoed the same, stating, "Intelligence indicated that the 3rd NVA Division was massing in the mountains and going to attack from the mountain area to the coast near the southern end of Quảng Ngãi Province, the AO for the 1-20th Infantry. [If they were successful] it would effectively cut off the five Northern provinces from the rest of South Vietnam." Alpha Company and the rest of the 1st Battalion, 20th Infantry would move back to the mountains in mid-September to take on a major role in this campaign.

In early September, the South Vietnamese government supported by Allied forces conducted a pacification program. Allied forces coordinated combat efforts in all four Tactical Zones. The intent - to search out the enemy and destroy their capabilities to wage war. Once areas were clear, local South Vietnamese governments, popular forces, police, and civil authorities screened local inhabitants to weed out VC sympathizers. The pacification initiative moved west to the smaller hamlets following the clearing of the larger cities. The program had controversial results at best.

Monsoons continued during the month of September. Mud knee deep and swiftly moving streams hampered movement in the bush, but it did not stop 3rd platoon and Alpha Company from their Search and Clear operations originating from firebase LZ Liz.

The layout of LZ Liz was similar to other forward firebases, except there were two hills, one sheared off to make it flat, a perfect location for an Observation Post (OP). Due to the flat contour of the saddle, it acted as a Pick-up Zone (PZ). LZ Liz included a Command Post (CP), mess hall, munitions storage, medical facility, artillery battery, and a radar system. Soldiers slept on cots in fortified bunkers, sandbags all around. Withered stumps and bare hilltops stripped of vegetation from Agent Orange framed the firebase perimeter and afforded unobstructed fields of fire for defensive lines. Razor wire surrounding the firebase afforded protection from sappers and enemy attacks.

On a sweep, 3 September, Ray's platoon found signs of Việt Cộng presence. That evening they set up an NDP with ambush sites in six locations less than a Klick northeast of the hamlet Pho Hoe on the Song Con River. With fields of fire identified and Claymore mines in position, they settled in for the night. It was quiet that evening with no insurgent contact.

From 4 through 7 September, Ray's platoon provided security for LZ Liz. Each evening, rituals preceded the patrols–Soldiers cleaned their weapons and packed plenty of ammunition, food and water. They donned their field caps and humped three to three and a half Klicks south of LZ Liz's perimeter to set up multiple ambush sites. On the 7th, Ray's platoon engaged one VC carrying sensitive documents and maps. They killed the insurgent and evacuated the documents to LZ Bronco, the Battalion TOC.

On the 8th, based on a suspected VC sighting, Alpha Company conducted a combat assault nine kilometers south of LZ Liz and less than a Klick west of the Song Phu Phone River. First pickup was 0645 hours, and the last chopper landing was 0707 hours. The LZ was cold, no enemy contact upon landing.

It was 1404 hours. Ray's platoon observed a woman carrying a large quantity of food, probably rice. They detained and questioned the suspect. Three males walking behind the female quickly fled the area without capture. While 1st and 2nd platoon returned to LZ Liz, Ray's platoon set up a NDP with three ambush sites near their original insertion point. The NDP provided good fields of fire. The evening turned out to be uneventful with no enemy contact.

They returned to LZ Liz the next morning where Ray's platoon and the balance of Alpha Company provided security for the firebase. For the next six days, Ray's platoon saw little action.

G3 at America's headquarters originally planned Operation Champaign Grove as a relief operation for the Special Forces CIDG Camp Detachment A-104 located in Hà Thanh, situated along a strategic supply route that led from the mountains to Quảng Ngãi City. It was conceived as a three-phase campaign and later broadened to include Search and Clear operations in the western part of Quảng Ngãi Province as military intelligence learned there was a concentration of enemy forces in the Song Re Valley south of the Sông Trà Khúc Horseshoe.

Under Command Headquarters Taskforce Galloway, American Division, the 11th Light Infantry Brigade commanded by Colonel Oran K. Henderson, the 4th and 6th ARVN Regiments and 1st Battalion, 1st Air Cavalry would act as a blocking force to disrupt enemy supply-lines and prevent an impending attack on Quảng Ngãi City. The 22nd NVA Regiment (part of the 3rd NVA Division) with an estimated strength of 1,200 troops and the balance of the 3rd NVA Division with an estimated troop strength of 2,300 were moving into the AO. Intel also indicated that the 2nd VC Main Force Regiment was operating northwest of Quảng Ngãi City.

The Hà Thanh Special Forces (SF) Camp, twenty-five kilometers west of Quảng Ngãi City, had been under siege since 23 August. Horrific enemy mortar fire and 122 mm rocket attacks pummeled the camp. The NVA overran OP 4, despite the heavy bombardment by friendly Tactical Air support. This Observation Post was critical as it overlooked the SF Camp and surrounding terrain. Several attempts to retake the OP failed.

A Naval bombardment called in by Sergeant Ivan Davis from the battleship New Jersey sitting off the coast of Quảng Ngãi Province struck targets on the west side of the camp. *"Man,"* he said, "When one of those shells crosses over, what an eerie sound. The ground shook just like an Arc Light [B-52] Strike."

Brigade surveillance spotted Soviet made NVA PT-76 light reconnaissance tanks southwest of the camp, and once again, Air Force tactical aircraft struck targets between OP's 2 and 3, destroying the enemy tanks. A Mobile Strike Force Company reinforced the besieged Green Berets and prevented the enemy from reaching the main part of the camp.

It was 13 September, two days before the scheduled combat assault to the Hà Thanh SF Camp. Conscious of time and the pending mission on his mind, Ray wrote my parents and Sandra a letter. "I haven't written in a while so I thought I'd better let you know what's happening. Actually, this area has been quiet although we got a few [insurgents] the other day. Sunday we will be moving northwest to Minh Long and Hà Thanh where the area has been under siege for a few days. We should be up in that area for a little while. It's just northwest of Đức Phổ near Quảng Ngãi [City]."

That would be the last letter my family would receive from Ray.

On the fourteenth, they stood down, recharged and refit.

That evening at 1800 hours, the battalion TOC received confirmation of rumors from the Hà Thanh SF Camp that several hundred NVA from the 3rd Division were massing northwest of Hà Thanh and closing in on the SF Camp. Delta Company, 1-20th had already been airlifted to the area at 1300 hours prior to receiving the news.

According to reports from Battalion S2 (Military Intelligence), once again NVA tanks massed outside of the SF Camp. "We received truckloads of [M72] Light Anti-tank Weapons (LAW)," said Lieutenant McNown. Each Soldier in the company received a shoulder-fired LAW. On every mission, each platoon normally carried 3-4 LAWs, primarily to use against bunkers and fixed installations. This, however, was an extraordinary situation.

After chow, Captain Adams summoned all platoon leaders and platoon sergeants to the CP for a briefing. A large topographical map of Quảng Ngãi Province covered the wall of the CP. A sheet of Plexiglas overlaid the map, and florescent lights framed the edges.

Adams outlined the overall mission for the 11th Brigade: to find, fix, and destroy elements of the 3rd NVA Division concentrated along the Sông Re Valley and south of the Sông Trà Khúc horseshoe, interdict supply routes to Quảng

Ngãi City, and eliminate the threat of an attack on the city. As Adams marked up the Plexiglas covered situation map with a grease pencil, the platoon leaders and platoon sergeants jotted down notes. Ray transcribed the details in his small black notebook that he carried into each battle.

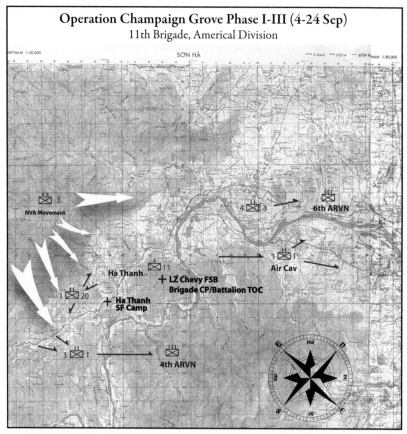

Illustration of Operation Champaign Grove 11th Brigade and NVA Troop movement

As I leafed through Ray's musty smelling black book with pages bronzed from age, I visualized Captain Adams outlining the mission for Alpha Company and the 1-20th. Alpha Company will be on the left flank, Charlie Company on the right. Delta Company will be in the lead and Bravo Company in the rear. From our insertion point at the Special Forces Camp, we will sweep in a northerly direction toward Câo Nguyên for about two Klicks, crossing the Song Xy Dieu River. We will continue north for about five Klicks to grid 38, 73; then southwest toward Xã Ky Mao. We will use "recon by fire" during our combat sweeps to flush out suspicious or suspected enemy positions, ten rounds maximum.

Third Battalion, 1st Infantry Regiment is currently in place and will operate on the left flank of the 1-20th as we sweep the valley. The 4th Battalion, 3rd Infantry Regiment already in place will sweep north of the Tha Khuc River with the 1st Battalion, 1st Air Calvary and drive east to link up with elements of the 6th ARVN Regiment. Radio frequency to the battalion CP will be 43.25.

Papa Oscars (Points of Origin) for this mission will be grids 36, 72 TREE; 37, 67 DIRTY; 41, 66 COKE; and 33, 68 LOVE. Papa Oscars (POs) were reference map grids for elements of Alpha Company to pinpoint their locations throughout the mission in the AO.

Adams continued. The terrain in the AO is composed of mountains and hill masses covered by dense underbrush and single canopy forest that will afford the enemy safe movement and cover. Undergrowth, grassland, and rice paddies cover the low hills and valleys. In this area, cover and concealment for the enemy will be limited to paddy dikes, road embankments, and riverbanks.

In the mountains and foothills, the terrain will restrict our movement. It will be slow, and visibility, observation, and fields of fire will be severely restricted. In the lowlands, we can move more easily, and visibility will be good.

The Battalion Command Post and TOC will move from LZ Bronco to LZ Chevy, high atop Nui Giap, four kilometers northeast of the Special Forces Camp. This will provide good observation of the AO. Call sign for the CP will be "Mint."

Captain Adams continued his briefing. B-Battery, 1st Battalion, 82nd Artillery equipped with 155 mm rounds and D-Battery, 6th battalion, 11th Artillery firing 105 mm rounds, both located at LZ Chevy, will support the 11th Brigade. The 7th USAF tactical aircraft group will support us operating sorties on suspected NVA targets.

The 14th Aviation Battalion flying AH-1 Cobra gunships will provide close in support. Cobras provided enormous firepower for ground troops. Depending on the configuration, they could pack 7.62 mm mini-guns, 40 mm grenade launchers, or more commonly, 2.75-inch rockets, two pods per gunship, nineteen rockets in each pod.

As Captain Adams outlined the elements of the mission on the map, the florescent lights around its edges cause his markings to glow, adding to the aura and mystique of the mission. Also on the map was the 3rd NVA Division's current location and their anticipated easterly and southeasterly movement out of the mountains toward Quảng Ngãi City.

Adams asked for questions and closed the mission briefing.

Alpha Company would leave for Hà Thanh tomorrow (the 15th) at first light.

That evening Ray and his platoon sergeant prepared their platoon and reviewed the mission with squad leaders Matheson, Williams, Merithew, and

Shepard. Lieutenants McNown and Burgraff, platoon leaders for 2nd and 1st platoons did the same.

Ray developed a close relationship with his platoon sergeant and squad leaders, largely built on trust and respect. The effect he had over his men was not for personal gain or braggadocio. Ray encouraged open communications and discussion, particularly before a mission as large and important as this. Glynn Hale supported this approach to leading. "There should be no doubt in a Soldier's mind that what he [or she] is asked to do is in his [or her] and the organization's best interest. A superior must know he [or she] is receiving information and opinions that are accurate and stripped of nuances for personal gain."

The day of the briefing, Ray's RTO departed for R&R; he would miss this mission. Ray selected Specialist Fourth Class Bill McAlarney as his RTO. His call sign suffix would be "three-six tango." McAlarney and his comrades knew the mission would be different; it was real, and they sensed it. They would not be fighting Việt Cộng insurgents. They would engage the NVA, a well-trained and well-equipped fighting force bound and determined to avenge the tactical defeats they suffered during the first two phases of *Tet*. Based on the Intel, McAlarney and his comrades also knew the prospects of encountering a far superior force in numbers would be very high. McAlarney said," Most of us wrote home thinking it was going to be our last writing."

Bill grew up in Darien, a small community on Connecticut's "Gold Coast" and was drafted in January 1968 while attending Norwalk Community College. After his tour of duty in Vietnam, he completed his education at the University of Arizona. He lived in Vermont for four years and eventually relocated back to Darien where he started his own construction company building homes for celebrities like Howard Cosell and Michael Bolton.

On a mission such as this, the fighting Soldier carried sixty-five to seventy pounds of ammunition and equipment while humping through the jungle, up and down mountains and across streams.

Matheson recalled, "On the pistol belt we carried at least two ammunition pouches that held five to six loaded magazines (seventeen to eighteen, 5.56 mm rounds per magazine) or loose ammo on "stripper clips," ten rounds per clip, fifteen to twenty clips per pouch." In addition, riflemen carried an M16 weighing 8.2 pounds fully loaded and one bandoleer with M16 ammo, six to seven magazines across the chest and another one in their rucksack; plenty of water, at least two quart size canteens, sometimes three; plus iodine tablets. Add to that a bayonet and scabbard; field dressing pouch; fragmentation grenades weighing almost a pound each, at least two, often times four; and a compass if you were a squad leader or higher in rank.

All would carry a LAW weighing five and a half pounds; some would carry M18A1 Claymore mines with wire and detonator; and a linked chain of 100 7.62 mm M60 machine gun rounds. On this mission, some would carry 81 mm mortar rounds weighing fifteen pounds, each distributed among the squads.

Each grenadier (two per rifle squad) carried an M79 grenade launcher commonly known as "Thumper" or "Blooper." It fired a 40 mm high explosive shell and had an effective range of 350 meters. For close order engagements, grenadiers carried rounds containing fléchettes, pointed steel projectiles with finned tails for stable flight.

On the Ruck they carried more water, shovel, flashlight, poncho, and one to two smoke grenades for spotting if they were a squad leader or higher. Inside the Ruck, they carried a poncho liner, clothing, plenty of socks, foot powder, insect repellent, C-Rations, various hygiene items, and rifle cleaning kit.

In lieu of an M16 Ray carried a CAR-15, an assault carbine particularly effective for close-in fighting. Incorporating a telescoping shoulder stock, it was shorter and lighter in weight. Ray also carried a .45 caliber pistol, as did the M60 gunner and assistant gunner.

Later that evening Captain Adams, Lieutenant McNown, Lieutenant Burgraff, and Ray went to the makeshift club. When all platoons were in from the field, which was rare, they would go there to talk about girls, cars, and previous combat missions. "It had a small bar, some tables and chairs," said McNown. He remembered Ray talking about his Austin Healey. It was rare they did this, as one or more platoons were typically in the field on missions or pulling perimeter security.

They also talked about the eminent combat assault to the Special Forces Camp in Hà Thanh. Little did they know this assault would involve three brutal firefights against known elements of the North Vietnamese Army's 3rd Division, the worst clashes Alpha Company would see since the assault on Hill 532 in May at the battle of Nui Hoac Ridge, prior to Ray's arrival.

In these horrific battles, there would be several wounded Soldiers and loss of life, over the course of eight days.

Chapter 10

Tragedy at Câo Nguyên

"You will never do anything in this world
without courage. It is the greatest quality in the mind
next to honor."

Aristotle

The NVA were on the move, several hundred spotted traveling in a south-easterly direction out of the mountains in the northwest sector of the AO. The Intel was accurate. They were headed toward Hà Thanh.

Prior to "lift-off," a Chaplain unexpectedly appeared at the pick-up zone. "It was a beautiful day on the 15th," recalled Lieutenant McNown. White irregular shaped clouds appeared, suspended in the blue sky. While standing on his jeep, the Chaplin said a prayer for the troops and wished them well. "A bad omen," said McNown, knowing Alpha Company would shortly embark for Hà Thanh.

Alpha Company was ready to go, periodically searching the sky, patiently waiting for the Helos. The mission briefing fresh in their minds, they waited at the PZ nearly all day. At 1600 hours in the afternoon, the battalion TOC advised Captain Adams that the pick-up was postponed until the following day. They humped back over a small rise to where the bunkers were located, had a hot meal, rested, and waited for a "go."

That evening Captain Adams was able to get a hold of some liquor. Sergeant First Class Wright, the field First Sergeant, Ray, Brad, First Lieutenant Douglas Falck, Doc Bushey, and John relaxed in the makeshift club. Ray lit up a cigar. "We had a pretty good buzz on," said McNown. He remembered Ray explaining the game of lacrosse and its aggressive nature. They also talked about where they were from and where they grew up. John said, "I found out more about

Captain Adams, Ray, Doug, Doc, and Brad than I knew the entire time I was in Vietnam." "That's where I really got to know LT Enners," said Doc. "We talked quite a bit. I called him Sir, and he called me Doc."

They talked. Ray puffed on a cigar. They lingered and talked some more. "We didn't talk about the mission, only small talk," said Doc. It was a way to flush out their thoughts and release the stresses of war. Those moments are rare, particularly on the front lines. It also enabled the leadership of Alpha Company to get to know each other. That was essential for developing and maintaining an effective fighting unit.

"We were all pretty tense knowing we were going to Hà Thanh the next morning," said John–after all, the Special Forces Camp was under siege, and it would be their job to relieve the intense pressure on the camp from the fighting warriors of the 3rd NVA Division. Ray was very enthusiastic about the mission, the action and engaging the enemy, as was Captain Adams. Ray had the warrior type spirit.

This was no routine company-wide sweep. Ray knew that. Champaign Grove was a Brigade plus size operation involving more than 4,500 U.S. infantrymen plus tactical support units and ARVN fighting elements. Knowing Ray, he focused on the mission and prepared himself, mentally applying the skills he learned while in Vietnam and Ranger School to the eminent task. That would give him the confidence to lead his platoon in this operation. Over the course of his life, he met every challenge with intensity, enthusiasm, and determination, and this would be no exception.

The next morning, Monday the 16th, Alpha Company saddled up and humped back to the PZ. "It was early, right after breakfast, a little after sun up," recalled McNown. Ray's platoon (three rifle squads and a weapons squad) along with Captain Adams and the Company CP would lift off in the first wave of Hueys.

Platoon sergeants and squad leaders did a final check of each squad, tightening straps and ensuring all equipment was secure. Ray and Lieutenants McNown and Burgraff offered some words of encouragement to their platoon, careful not to invade the thoughts each Soldier embraced before a mission, for it was a personal world in which only they were familiar. Deep inside, each Soldier knew he might not return to base camp alive.

Third platoon loaded up. On start-up, the turbine-powered engines whined. The nose of each chopper dipped as it lifted off; debris and dust flew freely from the rotor wash. In a matter of minutes, Firebase Liz receded from view. The balance of Alpha Company to include the mortar platoon followed in CH-47 Chinooks.

The insertion point was fifty Klicks to the northwest, a twenty minute flight. In a rapid descent, Ray's UH-1 flared-in to land, as did the other "slicks" carrying elements of 3rd platoon. The skids touched down; the doors opened. In a matter of seconds, Captain Adams, Ray and the command team hopped out, crouching beneath the rotor blades. The balance of 3rd platoon's Hueys landed. Ray immediately signaled to his comrades to form a perimeter securing the LZ. It is Standard Operating Procedure on a combat assault—not only for the safety of the troops, but for the chopper crew also.

Chinooks carrying Alpha Company, first one, then two, then a third settled in, touching down first on their rear wheels, then the front. The ramps dropped, and with their heads lowered, the troops scurried out of the rear of the choppers. Having arrived prior to the main force of Alpha Company, Ray scouted the terrain and visually mapped out the company-wide perimeter so that as the "Chalks" arrived, 1st and 2nd platoon plus the weapons platoon could deploy quickly to their sectors. Chalk was a nickname derived from a practice used during World War II. Flight line personnel wrote aircraft flight numbers on the backs of paratroopers in chalk. It later became popular in Vietnam to designate helicopters, sometimes numbered in chalk, for a major combat assault.

Alpha Company completed the combat assault to the Sông Trà Khúc valley near the Hà Thanh SF Camp at 0850 hours. "We dug in on a hill," said Mc-Nown, "on the northwest end of the runway." It was on the same hill where they launched the attack on the NVA 22 September that freed OP-7.

Ray and Captain Adams were on the horn with Lieutenant Colonel Guinn receiving an update to their orders. Lieutenants McNown, Burgraff, and Ray briefed their squad leaders on the immediate mission - to locate and destroy an arms cache in the mountains about five Klicks north of their insertion point. There was NVA activity in the AO. "We could hear artillery firing in the distance as well as small arms fire," said McNown.

All companies of the 1-20th moved into their assigned sectors by 1300 hours. At 1430 hours, Captain Adams gave the order to move out. The weather was good and temperature moderate. They knew the mission would be greater than searching for the arms cache, and that added to the existing tension. What waited for them along the way was unknown. They would soon find out.

Cảo Nguyên, Tuesday 17 September

From their insertion point with Ray's platoon on point and rifles at the ready, Alpha Company started to the east and then headed north toward the hamlet of Cảo Nguyên. As the file humped through the bush, 3rd platoon alternating their

M-16s left and right, the pointman spotted Hồ Chí Minh sandal tracks. Dép lốp, as the locals call them, were made of recycled tire rubber and worn by the Vietnamese populace. They leave a distinct footprint, easy to track.

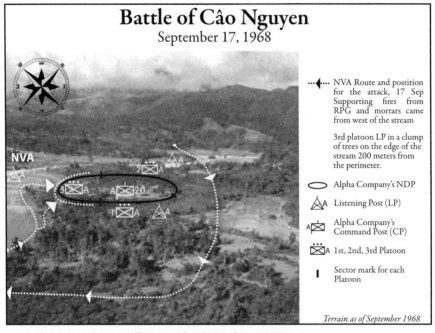

Battle of Câo Nguyen
September 17, 1968

⋯◄⋯ NVA Route and postition for the attack, 17 Sep Supporting fires from RPG and mortars came from west of the stream

3rd platoon LP in a clump of trees on the edge of the stream 200 meters from the perimeter.

◯ Alpha Company's NDP

◣A Listening Post (LP)

A◹ Alpha Company's Command Post (CP)

◹A 1st, 2nd, 3rd Platoon

| Sector mark for each Platoon

Terrain as of September 1968

Illustration for The Battle at Câo Nguyên

They approached a small hamlet that consisted of four or five Hooches. Several booby traps spotted near the hamlet raised the anxiety level of the lead squad–the unknown terror of the bush came in different forms, booby traps being one of them. It was a common practice by the VC and NVA to delay and disrupt movement by injuring or wounding friendly forces. The enemy made every effort to get GIs out of the bush, anyway they could.

There was no one in sight, which seemed strange. After disarming the booby traps, they pressed on, alert and determined to find the arms cache. Along the trail, they spotted several more sandal tracks and followed them over a hill and into the valley. Just as Ray's platoon completed their descent into the valley, they came to a stream that slowed the column. They noticed kids herding water buffalo in a nearby rice paddy on the other side of the stream.

"We started to pile up," said McNown, "so my platoon swung right. That put us on point with Captain Adams behind us." The staggered cluster of infantrymen began to straighten out as they continued on the trail.

The sky turned cloudy. "It started raining, I mean really raining," said Mc-Nown. The stream was deep and running fast, but a safe spot to cross was in view. Dusk was approaching. Tap ... tap ... tap. The sounds of the rain striking the foliage drowned out the distant roar of friendly artillery.

Alpha Company forded the stream and 2nd platoon picked up the trail once again. They followed the sandal tracks, not knowing the extent or intention of the enemy column. On point for 2nd platoon was Specialist Fourth Class Barney Kinnard III, a big blond-headed Soldier from Panama City, Florida. With raindrops bouncing off his steel helmet and water cascading off his helmet on to his nose, he continued to follow the trail, carefully clearing branches away from his face. He spotted several booby traps, hastily assembled and fixed. Realty set in and tension grew, Kinnard conscious of the crucial significance of every step.

Second Platoon swung out to the edge of the trees, and Ray's platoon once again took the lead. Deciding that the trail was too dangerous, Captain Adams called for all platoons to back track southwest and move around a finger of trees.

Darkness was moving in quickly, and the torrent of rain made visibility worse, perfect for an enemy ambush.

In an area with adequate tree cover, they established a NDP with Captain Adam's Command Post located near the center of the company perimeter. Nearby, the eight-man mortar crew set up in an open grassy area. The company perimeter occupied low flat ground, which is unusual. Doc Bushey said, "We normally establish a NDP on high ground."

Ray's sector (3rd platoon) had a stream to its west that ran north to south and rice paddies to its west between their perimeter and the stream. About ten meters from 3rd platoon's perimeter (along the tree line), there was a three to three and a half foot lateral drop off that ran the length of the paddies. Fields of fire to the north was good, but limited to the west and south due to thick vegetation and trees. Sergeant Matheson positioned his squad near the middle of 3rd platoon's sector. He recalled, "My squad didn't have good fields of fire, but we [dug] in." Sergeant Shepard, Weapons Squad Leader, positioned the two M60 machine guns, "staked," so they would not cause danger to other members of the platoon.

The M60, commonly known as "the pig" due to its weight and bulkiness, is a powerful belt-fed machine gun firing a 7.62 mm NATO cartridge. It fires 500-650 rounds per minutes at almost two and a half times the speed of sound.

Second platoon's sector was positioned north and east of the CP with good fields of fire to their front, but limited fields of fire where they tied in with 1st and

3rd platoon due to thick foliage and numerous trees. Lieutenant McNown positioned himself and his Radio Telephone Operator, Specialist Fourth Class Bob Sheen, on the northern side of the platoon's perimeter where his platoon tied in to Ray's right flank. Sergeant First Class Wright positioned his M60 machine guns and dug in on the far eastern part of the platoon perimeter.

First Platoon positioned themselves south and east of the CP. Fields of fire were similar to 2nd platoon. McNown recalled, "It took a while to figure out how to tie in with the other platoons flank because the foliage was very thick on either side."

The rain continued. "It rained so hard that we could not keep the sides of our foxholes from caving in," said McNown. Most of the Soldiers ended up with a shallow trench that barely provided any protection from small arms fire, grenades, or RPGs. As they dug in, they set up a shelter-half to shed the deluge of rain.

Lying in a wet, muddy foxhole was not a Soldier's idea of comfort on the battlefield. Then, again, finding comfort in the boonies seemed like a dream. You never knew what creatures were keeping you company. The thought of an ominous cobra, coral snake, or krate slithering over your body was enough to keep a Soldier on high alert, all night long.

Lieutenant McNown placed a three-man Listening Post (LP) in a cluster of trees about fifty meters northeast of the main body of his platoon. East of their perimeter, there was a trail running north to south, and the foliage was dense in some areas between the trail and their perimeter. In other areas, the foliage was sparse and open for good fields of fire.

Lieutenant Burgraff, leading 1st platoon, placed his LP in the trees south of the main body of the platoon at about fifty to sixty meters. A connecting trail that lay south of their position ran east to west toward the paddies.

Ray set up a six-man LP and ambush site on the east side of the stream in a small grove of trees 200 meters west of his platoon's perimeter. Squad Leaders Sergeants Matheson, Williams, and Merithew selected two men each to man the LP and ambush site. Sergeant Matheson chose Corporal Willie Hardy and Private First Class Richard Chambers. Sergeant Williams selected Specialist Fourth Class George Lee and one other. Sergeant Merithew chose Corporal George Shannon plus one other. All LPs were in place by 1800 hours and lanes established for Soldiers staffing the LPs to return to their respective platoon perimeters. Communications with the CP would be via a PRC-6.

The senior Forward Observer developed Artillery Pre-plans for both 105 mm and 155 mm howitzers from firebase Chevy. Ray and RTO Specialist Fourth Class

McAlarney periodically checked-in with the squad leaders and then settled in behind their perimeter line. Rotating shifts of surveillance maintained security.

"It continued to pour until about 0100 hours the next morning," recalled John. Soldiers poked their heads out of their dripping wet ponchos as they periodically awoke to the sounds of the falling rain. Under the shell of their poncho, their poncho liners kept them warm. "That worked quite well," said Matheson. "You could be soaking wet in a poncho liner, and your body heat would stay inside."

Cool, damp air followed the torrential rain. A heavy demonic layer of fog slowly blanketed the area, obliterating any visual signs of the stream and paddies to the west. No stars, no moon to light-up the black of the early morning. Visibility was virtually zero. What could be worse? The low-lying fog provided some concealment, but that works both ways. An eerie ghostly silence descended on Alpha Company's night defensive perimeter. Doc Bushey completed his one and a half hour radio watch monitoring the Listening Posts. He turned it over to another Soldier and went to sleep, boots on and within a short reach of his M16.

At about 0300 hours on the 17th, 2nd platoon's LP called-in.

In a soft whisper, Six, this is Lima Papa 2. This is Lima Papa 2. Come in Six. Over.

This is Six. Over.

Six, we got movement to our front. Over.

Roger that, Lima Papa 2. Hold your position. Out. The enemy were not visible, but the LP could hear the NVA moving in a southerly direction.

About forty minutes later, 1st platoon's LP called in and said they heard movement in their sector, moving east to west toward the paddy fields.

Third platoon's LP never reported in. Radio communications between the CP and the LP fell silent. Ray tried to reach them for a "Sit Rep" (situation report), but to no avail.

It was about 0400 hours. Shattering the morning silence, a grenade exploded on the east side of the company perimeter near where 1st and 2nd platoon tied in. "It was a ruse," said Captain Adams, merely an NVA probe. Alpha Company maintained their fire discipline–they did not engage, as it would have given away their position.

At about 0415 hours, second platoon's LP called in and said they were moving back to the perimeter. Lieutenant McNown could not reach Captain Adams by radio to get permission to pull in his LP. There was no response. He tried again; no response. McNown advised the LP to hold on a little longer. In the meantime, he sent two men to the Command Post to determine why the lapse in communications. The CP finally came on line. Adams said, "Affirmative. Pull in the LPs. Out."

Lieutenant McNown and Lieutenant Burgraff immediately withdrew their LPs by means of the previously established lanes. Ray's LP was silent. He knew there was a problem.

All was quiet, *deadly* quiet.

Within fifteen minutes, all hell broke loose directly in front of 3rd platoon's sector–not exactly the wake-up call that Ray's platoon was expecting. Thunderous bursts of enemy fire broke the silence of the early dawn. From a one meter high dike wall at the edge of the rice paddy and within ten meters of Ray's perimeter, Soviet made NVA RPD machine guns lit up the morning darkness. Doc Bushey awoke to the sounds and light show of the incoming fire. "It was dark, real dark, green tracers coming in." The NVA pounded Ray's position with the force of an iron fist. AK-47 bullets ripped into the earth, penetrated, and tore limbs off trees. Communists' hand grenades followed.

Supporting fire from rocket propelled grenades and mortars rhythmically pounded Alpha Company's perimeter from across the stream as did 7.92 mm rounds from MG-34 machine guns. That "told me in an instant exactly where their attack was coming from," said Captain Adams. Nazi Germany designed and manufactured MG-34s before World War II. During the fall of Berlin, the Russians captured selected models and provided them to the North Vietnamese Army.

Choosing selected squads from 1st and 2nd platoon, Adams set up a response element to sweep through the perimeter in the event the NVA broke through Ray's sector.

A belt-fed RPD firing 7.62 mm NATO rounds at twice the speed of sound continued to rake the area slightly to the right of Sergeant Matheson's squad. "It was dark, and you couldn't see anything," said Matheson. He was outside of his foxhole when the NVA lit up 3rd platoon's sector. Exposing himself to sure death, Matheson opened up. The rest of his squad opened up. He and his team laid down fire to gain fire superiority. "All I could see was the flash of my M16, I'm sure lighting me up as a target," said Matheson. He took cover.

"Cease fire." "Cease fire," yelled Matheson. *"Use grenades."*

Since the NVA were in hand grenade range, Matheson immediately told his squad to switch to grenades. "I threw every grenade I had," said Matheson. They can be effective, particularly at close range. The explosion and resulting concussion effect has the ability to disorient the enemy. It helped temporarily, but grenades did not stop the NVA and their reign of terror. Rounds continued to scorch the earth.

Like ghosts in the jungle, in the stone cold dark of the early morning and heavy fog, a suspected reinforced platoon or company size NVA force maneuvered up to the one meter high dike and moved laterally south to north, using it as cover to deliver their arsenal of fire.

During the firefight, a Soldier from Ray's ambush site ran back to the company perimeter. Filled with fear and in a state of panic, he managed to evade detection by the NVA and the horrific fire coming from 3rd platoon's sector. "It was a miracle that he was not killed," said McNown.

Gunners in Ray's weapons squad, conscious of overheating the barrels, rhythmically fired their M60 machine guns–swiveling left and right–attempting to gain fire superiority and trying to neutralize the NVA machine guns to their front. A string of red tracers from the steaming M60s ripped into the enemy position along the embankment. The NVA were not advancing. They were firing from their well-concealed position.

An enemy grenade exploded. Fragments hit one of Ray's gunners. The assistant gunner jumped onto the M60. The assistant gunner continued to fire on the enemy positions. Another grenade exploded. Shrapnel penetrated the assistant gunner's flesh and hit the M60. There were dents all over it, but it was still operable. Both Soldiers lay in their shallow and mud-filled trench.

Ray, recognizing that one of the M60s was silent, maneuvered to its position. Seeing that both men were wounded, he called for a medic. Instincts and training kicked in. Ray fired the M60, focusing on the enemy muzzle-flash, thwarting the enemy advance. With an onslaught of enemy firepower, the NVA zeroed in on both of 3rd platoon's M60 emplacements. "There was no doubt that the NVA was trying to overrun Ray's position," said McNown.

The firefight intensified in front of 3rd platoon's sector. Once again, they retaliated with grenades and heavy volleys of fire. The sound was deafening. Captain Adams called in gunships; they were in route. As the gunships closed in on the battleground, the flight commander aborted the mission due to the thick fog that obscured the battle site.

Captain Adams took the plastic covered handset from his RTO and called for a "fire mission." With the aid of the FO, artillery from LZ Chevy zeroed in on the NVA position along the embankment and "rounds were flying over our heads," said McNown. Flares lit up the area to spot the rounds. Due to the proximity of the NVA to 3rd platoon's position, the transmission to the Fire Direction Center included "Danger Close." Exploding rounds severed tree limbs as the HE shells were registered. Red-hot shards of shrapnel fell within Alpha Company's perimeter. Shallow foxholes provided little protection.

Adams recalled he never jumped into his foxhole; he did not know why–maybe because a shallow mud-filled foxhole offered little protection. He communicated with his platoon leaders from this vulnerable position. Artillery from firebase Liz pummeled the enemy position on the paddy dike twenty meters from 3rd platoon's position.

Lieutenant McNown reinforced his flank on the north side where 2nd platoon tied in with 3rd platoon. Second platoon received no direct fire; it was mostly harassing fire from RPGs in the paddy area.

Ray's platoon held the perimeter line. They had to. They could not allow the NVA to breach their sector and place other elements of Alpha Company in a more dangerous situation. It would have been disastrous.

As the dawn approached, after a two hour firefight, all was quiet; the NVA broke contact and disappeared across the rice paddies and stream heading northwest toward the mountains. Their tactics during this engagement were common. When the NVA fought, they were fierce–typically used "hit and run" tactics fearful of the firepower of friendly artillery, gunships, and Tactical Air Support.

McNown hastily surveyed 3rd platoon's sector and thought, "What a mess, the bodies and the duds." Members of Alpha Company swept the immediate area and found an M16, an NVA B40 infrared night scope, and the stock of an M79 grenade launcher broken and splintered. Smeared on the sight of the grenade launcher was the flesh of a Soldier's scalp.

Shell casings, 7.62 mm and 5.56 mm, were scattered along 3rd platoon's perimeter. "On one side of the paddy dike, there were Ak-47 shell casings, and on the other side M16 casings," said Doc Bushey, "They were close, really close." Unexploded Chinese Communist grenades littered the site. Chi Com grenades were not very reliable as the friction fuses sometimes failed to ignite; fifty percent of the grenades never exploded. "There were so many hand grenades exchanged, and we found at least a dozen duds afterwards; Chi Com grenades, too," said Adams.

Adams confirmed, Ray's LP and ambush site was clearly overrun, but prior to the firefight, there was no indication of enemy movement in front of 3rd platoon's sector. "Because we did not hear the NVA advancing, we assumed the ambush squad was killed by silent techniques," said McNown. The NVA never did attack either 1st or 2nd platoon's sectors, although there was a minor skirmish where 3rd platoon tied in to 1st platoon.

The NVA killed four of the six members from Ray's platoon that worked the LP and ambush site. Private First Class Willie C. Hardy, Specialist Fourth Class George Lee, and Private Richard A. Chambers were lying in the rice paddies

100 meters from 3rd platoon's perimeter, dead. The NVA carried off Private First Class George D. Shannon's body in a northwesterly direction.

No Soldier is left behind–it's an integral part of the military "code" that dates back to the wars of ancient Greece during the 8th Century BC–the acknowledgement that respect and honor should bestow a fallen Soldier serving the nation. As the fog lifted, elements of 3rd platoon, including Ray, McAlarney carrying his twenty-five pound PRC-25, Specialist Fourth Class Eugene Stevens, and Private First Class Gregory Kaminsky recovered the three bodies from the paddy. At that time of year, the rice paddies were emerald green with the fall crop. From a distance, it was difficult to spot the dead Soldiers, but a closer recon of the paddy revealed irregular shapes of blood red. They followed the NVA trail for about 900 meters and recovered Shannon's body.

The sight of the dead sickened all in the pit of their stomachs. "The stench of dead bodies is like nothing else you could imagine," said McAlarney. The NVA ambushed Ray's men as they returned to the perimeter from the LP and ambush site. One survived, wounded three times in the belly. Ray's M60 gunner and assistant gunner survived their wounds.

During the harrowing firefight, the NVA wounded ten brave Soldiers from 3rd platoon; two from 1st platoon, and three Forward Observers (FO) directing artillery fire. All were not admitted to the surgical hospital in the rear. Thinking back on the firefight, John commented, "What saved us were the pre-plans developed to enable accurate firing of the artillery."

"The 81 mm mortars were virtually useless," said McNown. "The base plates sunk into the ground about two feet due to the deluge of rain prior to the firefight."

Captain Adams indicated that it was the scariest night he had spent in Vietnam, considering his vast experience with the Special Forces near the Laotian border.

Captain Adam's RTO called in Medevacs for the dead and wounded as Doc Bushey and his team of medics attended to the wounded. Olive drab ponchos concealed the bodies of the dead. The Battalion TOC at LZ Chevy flew an FO out to the site of the engagement that same day. Adams also requested and received several replacements.

Ray's platoon suffered most of the casualties. "Ray was really upset," said John. "He was angry that he lost so many Soldiers and took that very hard as we all did." Ray took it personally, as would any leader. Ask any officer or NCO who has experienced combat, and they will tell you the most difficult burden to carry, the most devastating situation to deal with, is the loss of a Soldier in your command. What would Ray say in a letter to their parents? What would he say in a face-to-face conversation with the parents when his tour of duty concluded? How could he have prevented the loss of human life? I am sure those questions reverberated in his head. I am sure he blamed himself. As platoon leader, he was ultimately responsible for those men; that's how he thought.

The burden of losing Brothers in Arms does not diminish at the higher levels of command. "In combat you at some time will put your men at risk," said William Guinn. "That's the hardest thing I had to accept. Sooner or later you're going to lose some guys." It's a type of "passage," a rite of passage for a leader in combat, the agony of the inevitable transition (of some) from life to death.

Captain Adams redistributed the men to balance out the strength of each platoon. At 1045 hours that morning, exhausted and in need of resupply, they moved west across the rice paddies and stream, then into the hills in search of the NVA who dealt 3rd platoon the devastating blow that morning. With Ray's platoon on point, followed by 2nd platoon, then 1st, Captain Adams initially used "recon by fire," employing 105 mm howitzers to pave the way for the lead platoon, ensuring a minimum safe distance of 250-300 meters.

Ray took the losses that morning very hard, but as a Soldier *and a leader,* he had to deal with it. He had to get his emotions under control; there were others to watch over. He had to press on, focus on the mission at hand. There would be time to mourn the dead and wounded later. Ray was accustomed to both emotional and physical challenges. He would work harder the next day, the next, and the next. That's how he operated.

They came upon a series of hedgerows, most of them impenetrable. All three platoons came to a dead stop. They began to stack up, making them vulnerable to an enemy attack. It was 1215 hours. Captain Adams and 2nd platoon moved off to the left until they came upon a firebreak leading through a grove of trees. Anxiety levels grew, fingers on their selector switches moving rapidly from auto to safe to auto. At the top of the ridge, they spotted NVA Regulars about fifty meters away. Lieutenant McNown's platoon engaged, and as the NVA dispersed, 2nd platoon hit and killed three.

With all senses keenly in high alert mode, Ray's platoon moved ahead as 2nd platoon shifted left. The lead squad from 3rd platoon came upon a small NVA camp and spotted an enemy soldier sleeping in a hammock. "We blew him out of [the hammock] before he had a chance to move," said McAlarney. Not more than five minutes later, two NVA threw hand grenades and tried to evade, but a brief engagement by Ray's platoon resulted in two NVA KIA. From a distance,

Matheson could hear the AK-47 rounds flying overhead, making the characteristic sound, *Zip, Zip, Zip.*

Alpha Company pressed on, and at 1320 hours, they located spider holes, cooking fires, and an enemy ammunitions cache containing three B-40 RPG rockets with boosters, one launcher, several bangalore torpedo tubes, and several packs of rice. Near the same location, they found two AK-47; 2,200 AK-47 rounds; and six RPG rounds. This was a good find and more than likely were the supplies left behind by the NVA as they hastily made their way into the mountains. A Chinook airlifted the weapons and materials to LZ Chevy. They continued their Search and Clear sweep with no further finds.

That evening they established a NDP with sister companies Bravo and Delta while Charlie Company conducted a sweep in the nearby mountains. Choppers arrived with ammunition and much needed supplies. Matheson recalled, "Two men transferred into my squad due to the losses sustained that day."

Ray conducted an After Action Review (AAR) of the morning's harrowing firefight with his platoon sergeant and squad leaders. This was a common practice after a mission or firefight and a solid leadership practice. It typically included an intense debriefing and discussion on what the platoon did well, what they did not do well, and what changes were required for future missions. It was a way to flush out mistakes so they would not be repeated in future engagements. It enabled all to ask questions, give their opinions, and discuss issues in an open forum without regard for rank or position. Sometimes emotions caused discussions to become heated, but leaving egos "at the door" was a prime requirement. Unchecked egos would likely cause confusion and disruption. Loss of focus on the mission would result when those involved operated with personal agendas.

Once again, Ray briefed his squad leaders for the following day's mission. Daylight narrowed to darkness. Ambush sites deployed and C-Rations for dinner, they settled in for the night. Under the dim glow of his red-lens flashlight, Ray checked the map for tomorrow's mission. Alpha Company would head further south through the Sông Trà Khúc Valley to act as a "blocking force" for Charlie Company, who was sweeping out of the mountains.

In the early evening, the "pop" of NVA mortar tubes could be heard outside of Alpha's Company's perimeter. Explosions followed with negative results. The barrage was short lived. Except for the far off sounds of artillery, mortar, and sporadic small arms fire that echoed through the valley, the balance of the evening was tranquil without enemy harassing fire or contact.

The peaceful night and early morning, however, would give way to another horrific day.

Chapter Eleven

COURAGE UNDER FIRE

"Every man is bound to do something before he dies.
If it be that to which he is called, then death is but a sleep."

Unknown

Dawn slowly and quietly crept into Alpha Company's night defensive position. It was Wednesday, the 18th. A night's sleep succeeded in calming Ray from the events of the previous day, but the fire kindling in his heart did not stop the burning sensation of losing so many men.

Alpha, Bravo, and Delta Companies went in different directions, each conducting a "recon in force," a sweep of their assigned areas. "We were surrounded by hills and rice paddies, and off in the distance we could see part of the [Annamite Cordillera] Mountain Range," recalled McNown. The view of the mountains stretched to the horizon.

"The morning was quiet as [Alpha Company] moved towards [their] blocking position," said Matheson.

As Alpha Company headed south, they stopped at coordinates BS352690, one Klick southwest of Xã Ky Mao, and had lunch, a hot lunch, flown in from the rear. A Soldier's dream it was. Mess kits in hand, Ray's platoon lined up for chow. Ray and the other officers, of course, ate last. The morning was quiet without enemy contact, time for Alpha Company to collect their thoughts from the harrowing firefight near Cào Nguyên.

Thirty minutes later Alpha Company moved out, conscious the NVA were in the vicinity, but not knowing exactly where. "Locked and loaded" and with the safety selector lever in the "auto" position on their M16s, Ray's platoon led the way with Sergeant Matheson's squad on point. "Even as a short-timer, I always liked to be up front," said Matheson. Squad leaders made the choice as to who would take point. "That's a tough decision," he said. "Ray would delegate that decision to the squad leaders." Lieutenant McNown's platoon was in second position with Captain Adams and his CP following, and Lieutenant Burgraff's platoon followed behind Adams. They followed a trail to an outcrop of trees.

In single file formation five to ten meters apart, the men in Ray's platoon crossed the rice paddies at their narrowest point to limit their exposure. During this sweep, Ray positioned himself near the middle of his platoon where he felt he could best observe and tactically control the actions of his platoon. He frequently varied his position within the platoon depending on the necessity, the mission, and circumstances.

All was quiet, no one in sight, not even a water buffalo or a farmer tending his crops. That was odd, odd considering the time of year.

As they reached the north side of the paddies, they turned west hugging the tree line, temporarily seeking protection from an outcrop or finger of trees and dense brush. "There was a drop-off one and a half to two feet [high] and another drop-off thirty-foot further to our left," recalled Matheson. "The drop-off was dry, but the next one was wet." Walking on the paddy dikes was not a wise idea, as more than likely they were booby-trapped. His squad was still in the lead; Matheson walking slackman, ten meters behind his pointman.

The pointman, keenly alert for any unusual noises, was further to the left of where Sergeant Matheson was as Ray insured that the column of men was staggered every five to ten meters. They rounded the finger and continued to move in a westerly direction along the tree line. It was a typical sweep, and all was quiet.

About seventy-five meters from the outcropping and within five meters of the tree line, the pointman, straining his ears, suddenly stopped and sunk to a crouch position. He whispered to Matheson that he heard something in the thicket to his right. "I gave a halt signal to those behind me," said Matheson. As third platoon dropped to one knee, Matheson crouched forward a step or two for better visibility into the thicket and saw a shadow of what appeared to be a man about three to five meters to his front.

Just as 2nd platoon crossed the rice paddies and sought cover behind the thick foliage of the finger of trees, a loud burst of automatic weapons fire rang out from the tree line seventy-five meters west of Lieutenant McNown's position.

"AK-47 fire, six, seven, eight round burst," said Matheson. As his rifle flew out of his right hand, Matheson fell on his side and back. He was hit in the back of the right elbow, and the 7.62 mm round exited on the inside, leaving a six inch wide opening. "Had the Dink aimed carefully from the distance he was from me, he could have filled me full of holes," he said. Matheson was so close to the NVA soldier, he could have looked down the barrel of the AK-47.

"All hell broke loose," said McNown. The once silent thicket exploded with enemy machine gun and small arms fire. From the rear of the paddy, Doc Bushey could hear the thicket explode. "The fire was horrendous," he said. He, Captain Adams, and the rest of the Company CP maneuvered left so Adams could have a better view to maneuver the platoons against the enemy.

Blood pulsating through his arteries, the pointman dove behind the nearest embankment and returned fire immediately. "My squad ran to the first drop-off and returned fire," said Matheson. They dumped everything they had into the tree line. "I looked at my arm, grabbed it with my left hand, and pushed it against my side to try and stop the bleeding."

"I was thinking: What am I going to do? Should I crawl out?" The NVA was no more than three meters away. "If I crawled out, they would see me." Did the NVA soldier think Sergeant Matheson was dead? So many questions; so many thoughts went through his mind. The best he could do for the moment was shield himself from the hellacious storm of bullets coming from the thicket.

Every second counted. "I pulled myself closer to the drop-off so they were less likely to see me. For the next ten minutes, no one could reach me." Bullets ripped through the paddies.

One of Ray's squads pushed into the thicket and tried to lay down suppressive fire, but the intense discharge of the enemy onslaught repelled their advance.

Members of 2nd platoon dropped their rucksacks behind the outcropping (finger) of trees, and Lieutenant McNown, along with seven members of his platoon, moved into the tree line and then forward on the right flank from the covered position. As they advanced through the thick underbrush, they spotted spider holes and fresh fires left by the NVA. "We were moving as fast as we could," recalled McNown, "watching our flanks as we advanced."

As he was moving through the finger of trees, McNown recalled, "I was behind the pointman, and the rest of the platoon was in a single file because of how thick the wooded area was; thorns and vines covered the area." He requested a count. There were only seven of McNown's platoon members behind him. He should have had twenty-five. Sergeant First Class Wright had taken two squads and the two M60 machine gun crews and maneuvered left of the finger of trees to support Ray's platoon.

Battle of Xã Ky Mao
Firefight September 18, 1968

+ Location where Ray was hit BS 353692   *Terrain as of September 1968*

Illustration of Firefight at Xã Ky Mao

As McNown and his men advanced through the finger of trees, they abruptly withdrew as the NVA maneuvered around them. The enemy automatic weapons fire intensified.

From a covered position south of the paddies, Lieutenant Burgraff and 1st platoon quickly moved across the narrow stretch of paddies behind the outcropping of trees and released their rucksacks.

"I could not get my right arm free from the rucksack strap," said Sergeant Matheson. "There was no release on that side, and the strap was under my right arm, which I was pressing against my body to stem the bleeding." He finally reached the strap on the left and released it.

"My adrenaline was rushing. I don't recall feeling any pain."

As he lay on his back, Matheson could hear a whistling sound as the Chi Com grenades flew over his head. Grenades were exploding all over. His squad responded, throwing grenades into the tree line. Matheson's wound compounded his problem. "I couldn't return fire or pull the pin on a grenade–It seemed like [an] eternity." He lay still, bleeding, a track of fresh blood seeping through the sleeve of his lower right arm.

Captain Adams grabbed the plastic covered handset from his RTO and pressed the "push to talk" button. *"Three-six, you must get your squad leader back.*

I'll send a trailing platoon around and flank the hedgerow." Ray positioned his platoon to lay down a base of fire for the maneuver platoon. Lieutenant Burgraff maneuvered 1st platoon around the outcropping of trees to support 3rd platoon and the machine gun crews from 2nd platoon.

Under a hail of bullets, Ray crawled forward through the paddy field from 100 meters back. He leaped over an intervening dike and reached Sergeant Matheson's squad and Sergeant Williams, Squad Leader 1st squad, who was about twenty meters from Matheson.

The gunfire from the tree line intensified. Return fire from Alpha Company escalated, spraying the thicket, attempting to gain fire superiority.

Without regard for his own life, Ray made two attempts to reach Sergeant Matheson, each attempt thwarted by enemy grenades, machine gun, and automatic weapons fire. Several moments passed. From the safety of a covered position, Ray regrouped his three squads and advised Captain Adams of his plan to rescue Matheson.

Ray maneuvered one squad toward the right flank about twenty meters from the enemy position. He maneuvered another squad further toward the left where they could lay down suppressive fire. The two M60 crews and two squads from 2nd platoon under the direction of Platoon Sergeant Wright maneuvered into position to best support this bold and final attempt.

Without reticence and adrenaline pumping unleashed, Ray's voice came on the radio. *This is three-six Actual. This is three-six Actual. I'm moving!*

"Out of nowhere I heard this incredible barrage of fire," recalled Matheson. "It sounded like everyone in the company opened up. There was so much firepower. It was so intense, it would have awakened the dead." It was deafening, Alpha Company pouring fire three to five meters inside the tree line. "Lieutenant Enners must have had the M60 gunners brought up, because it sounded like M60 machine guns. And, he would have wanted them up there. It makes a difference [in the firepower] when you have an M60."

"I bent back toward the rear of the paddy and saw Lieutenant Enners come over the drop-off in a crouched position with his [CAR-15] in his right hand, shooting as he ran. As he moved toward me, he had his left arm stretched out." Matheson knew what that meant.

"I know what went through my mind at the time; it scared me. If the NVA was still in the thicket, and Lieutenant Enners was going to pull me back into the open, I would be exposed to enemy fire." There was no time for Matheson to challenge what came next.

"I put my left arm out and [Lieutenant Enners] grabbed it, and he pulled me straight back. His clinched hand was as strong as steel. My arm came out of my rucksack. I was waiting for something to happen because I was exposed. He pulled me back to the next drop-off, which was three feet high." Due to the suppressing fire laid down by members of 1st, 2nd (platoon minus), and 3rd platoon, Sergeant Matheson did not suffer any additional injuries.

"I sat with my back against the drop-off, and a medic rushed toward me to render first-aid," recalled Sergeant Matheson. "Lieutenant Enners was stooping over me." Matheson's heart still racing, a degree of calm replaced anxiety and gloom. The medic stabilized Matheson's wound and injected him with morphine. He helped Matheson to a safe location towards the rear of the paddy field. "As they carried me back across the dikes, I noticed my mouth felt incredibly dry. I couldn't get enough water." He was feeling the effects of the morphine.

A Dustoff appeared ten minutes later, and Matheson, with some assistance, boarded the chopper and took off immediately. Matheson said, "I thought to myself, it's over for me." The Medevac carrying Sergeant Matheson landed at the Special Forces Base Camp in Hà Thanh.

It never shut down. He wondered what was going on. The door gunner told him they were going back to the firefight; more wounded, he said.

They lifted-off immediately.

Heart pounding, Ray reorganized his men and prepared to assault the tree line. He and Sergeant Kermit Williams moved two squads further to the right flank short of the tree line to within fifteen meters of the NVA so they could lay down cover fire. No more than twenty meters from the enemy position DeVincent unloaded eleven of his fourteen magazines into the tree line.

As bullets flooded the paddies, Ray and Williams rose to a half-crouch position to maneuver closer to the NVA position. A radio transmission stunned Alpha Company. The radio crackled. *Three-six is down! Three-six is down!"*

Seconds later, DeVincent recalled, "A guy next to me yelled, *Grenade!* I yelled, *Where?* He yelled it again. *Grenade!"* DeVincent moved to his left, saw the grenade; it exploded, lifting him into the air and causing him to land on his back. The explosion knocked him out, however, only for a moment. He woke up and fortunately suffered no wounds. "It was a concussion grenade, not a frag grenade," he said.

Knowing Ray was down, but not knowing the extent of his wounds, Captain Adams placed Sergeant First Class Wright temporarily in charge of 3rd platoon. The intense fire had Ray's platoon pinned down just outside of the tree line. In a gutsy move, with Lieutenant Burgraff's platoon providing supporting fire, elements of 3rd platoon assaulted the tree line, but the NVA thwarted their advance. Third platoon and 2nd platoon's weapons squad reluctantly withdrew forty meters toward the rear of the paddies.

Lieutenant McNown and 2nd platoon moved along the tree line, trying to get to Ray and Sergeant Williams, but could not do so. "The enemy fire was so thick that as we advanced to where Ray was hit, we had to pull back," said John.

He and Platoon Sergeant Wright pulled their elements further back behind the outcropping.

Artillery was not an option at that moment as 2nd platoon was too close to the enemy position. McNown would try one more assault. He reorganized his men near the wood line into three files. They would move in parallel through low growing vines and thorns and force the NVA into the paddies where elements of 3rd and 1st platoons could engage them. Squad Leader Sergeant Maestas was leading the file closest to the paddies; McNown, the file in the middle; and Wright, the inside flank column. McNown said, "It got so thick, we were crawling."

As Sergeant Maestas advanced, he threw grenades into each spider hole. Camouflaged behind thick foliage, an NVA shot Maestas in the shoulder. He was down–and then fatally injured with multiple "frag" wounds from an exploding grenade. Shrapnel from grenades hit several members of second platoon.

"As the Medevac helicopter approached the landing site, I could hear the bullets zipping through the open door of the chopper," recalled Sergeant Matheson. He pressed his body against the vibrating floor of the Helo, minimizing his exposure to the incoming fire. The LZ was "hot," NVA directing fire on the Medevac.

Upon landing, Matheson noticed six or seven wounded Grunts lying on the ground. Some required assistance and others jumped in. They lifted-off immediately in route to the 2nd Surgical Hospital in Chu Lai. Matheson was not aware that Ray received multiple wounds. Wounded twice during his combat tour, Matheson did not return to the battlefield. For him the winds of war faded to calm.

★ ★ ★

"Lieutenant Colonel Guinn, Battalion Commander, in his "Charlie-Charlie" (Command and Control) helicopter wanted us to pop smoke so he could see where the engagement was," said Lieutenant McNown. They popped smoke.

Due to the intense fire from the tree line, Captain Adams came on the radio. *"Pull back!"* he ordered. *"Pull back!"* All three platoons retreated across the paddies. Captain Adams requested artillery fire.

Lieutenant Colonel Guinn hesitated firing artillery because Ray, Sergeant Williams, and Sergeant Maestas might still be alive. Captain Adams asked for a confirmation of the status of Ray and Sergeant Williams. One Soldier responded and said neither was moving.

"I knew that my squad leader was dead," said McNown.

Machine gun fire fatally wounded both Ray and Sergeant Williams. Some say Sergeant Williams was hit first, and Ray maneuvered to his aid–and suffered the same fate. McAlarney was closest to Ray at the time and remembered as they both rose to advance against the NVA, they fell mortally wounded at the same time. He said, "[They] both died instantly."

Assured that all three men were dead, Lieutenant Colonel Guinn gave Captain Adams the OK to call in artillery on the enemy position. Adams chose eight inch HE shells. They were more accurate and more devastating.

A marking round from LZ Chevy soared into the CP. "It almost wiped out the Command Post," said Adams. Luckily, it was a dud. As it landed, the "thumping" sound scared the hell out of Adams. It left a hole in the ground six foot deep by four foot wide and splattered mud all over everyone. He immediately contacted the Fire Direction Center and redirected the artillery fire.

The screeching sound of the artillery filled the air. With rounds flying over Alpha Company's position, the artillery strike pummeled the hedgerow. The incessant roar of shells exploding calmed the nerves of Alpha Company's fighting best. The shelling was powerful; it was devastating. It lasted several minutes.

With Ray fatally wounded and Burgraff wounded in the leg, Adams placed 3rd platoon in reserve and 1st platoon under Sergeant First Class Wright. McNown and Wright maneuvered their platoons across the rice paddies and along the paddy dike toward the suspected enemy position. They opened up, short bursts of M16 and M60 fire.

A radio transmission bellowed, *"Cease fire! Cease fire!"* Lieutenant McNown could see that the NVA had abandoned their position and dispersed.

"The doctors numbed my arm with some type of electric gadget," said Sergeant Matheson. They positioned his arm where Matheson could see it and scraped what appeared to be plastic along the wound. They asked him if he could feel it. Even though he could not, Matheson told the doctor he could. "It accomplished what I wanted because they then put me out cold."

When Sergeant Matheson woke up, the first person he saw was his previous Platoon Sergeant, Sergeant First Class Dela Cruz. Dela Cruz heard what happened and told him that both Sergeants Williams and Maestas had died. He also broke the news about Ray. The impact on Matheson was not immediate, the morphine dulling his senses.

Sergeant Matheson spent two days in Chu Lai and relocated temporarily to Cam Rahn Bay, awaiting a flight to Japan. He received additional surgical procedures on the 24th and his arm placed in a cast. "My arm was a bit swollen and quite sore, but it was still there and quite alive," said Matheson.

★ ★ ★

Captain Adams pulled 1st and 3rd platoons back to high ground, a small hilltop one klick southwest of the battle site to set up an NDP. Not knowing whether the NVA would counter-attack, Doc Bushey said, "We stayed awake all night long."

It was getting dark, around 1900 hours. Captain Adams walked over to the tree line where the firefight took place. He and McNown found Ray and Sergeant Williams rather quickly. Locating Sergeant Maestas was more of a challenge as the lack of light and thick underbrush concealed his body. Members of 2nd platoon took the bodies across the rice paddies to a small grass covered hummock surrounded by trees. Doc Bushey recalled, "We laid them on the ground toward the right side of the hill." Out of respect, they covered their bodies with olive drab ponchos. Doc recalled, "It was my most vivid memory of Vietnam, those three bodies lying on the side of the hill. I was just sitting there looking at them. They were all my friends." Doc had been on many night ambushes with Maestas and respected him. Doc said, "He was really gung ho."

Adam's RTO called for a dustoff.

For Lieutenant Colonel Guinn, that day was chaotic. The 3rd NVA Division had platoon and company size forces all over the AO. "I went through five helicopters that day," he recalled. "One shot down. One went down for maintenance. Two others received enemy small arms fire and went back for maintenance. I finished the night with the one that pulled Ray's body out."

Guinn told Adams to abort the previously called dustoff. Guinn wanted to resupply Alpha Company with ammunition and pull the bodies out. He headed for the battle site with the battalion S2, Captain Caravalho.

It was about 2230 hours. There was a familiar silence in the dark of night, except for the distant *whop, whop, whop* of Guinn's "bird" easily heard by McNown and Bushey. The approaching Helo circled the rice paddy searching for a location to set down.

Guinn called Captain Adams on the radio and asked, "Can you find a clearing?" Adams said, "There's one big enough."

Guinn said, "Give us some light and we'll come in."

After spotting the light, Guinn pointed to the small clearing below where the three motionless bodies lay and asked his pilot. "Can you get in there?" The pilot responded, "Affirmative."

Bright lights shining down on the ruffled ponchos, Guinn's helicopter slowly descended through the canopy of trees slashing leaves as they went in. As the chopper set down on the grassy knoll toward the rear of the paddy fields, "The rotor wash blew the ponchos off," said Doc Bushey.

Lieutenant Colonel Guinn has never forgotten the look on Captain Caravalho's face as they loaded Ray's body on the helicopter. "I can still see his face," said Guinn, "a look of sorrow and disbelief."

Upon lift-off, the tall grasses danced from the turbulence of the rotor blades. The Helo carrying Ray, Sergeant Williams, and Sergeant Maestas was bound for Đức Phổ. "It was the worst day of my life, mostly because we had to carry them back to the dustoff location," said Lieutenant McNown. "Captain Adams thanked me for staying with Ray."

"Both of my machine gun crews were hit with shrapnel from grenades," said McNown. Private First Class Kenneth Watson, Sergeant Frederick Ragland, and Private First Class Joseph Scott received serious wounds from fragmentation grenades. Several others received wounds from small arms and machine gun fire.

Sergeant First Class Wright took over 1st platoon. Lieutenant Colonel Guinn returned to the battalion TOC at LZ Chevy.

Due to darkness, Alpha Company did not sweep the area for dead NVA; they would search tomorrow. Adams assembled the remnants of Alpha Company, established an NDP one klick from the battleground, and set up tight security, unsure if the NVA would counterattack.

As the black of the early morning turned to gray and gray turned to light, Bravo Company searched the hedgerow and found twenty-one NVA bodies–a good body count to report, perhaps, but at the expense of losing three brave American Soldiers.

First Lieutenant Douglas Falck flew in by helicopter to take over 3rd platoon. After two days of intense firefights, Alpha Company was severely short of troops. Airlifted to the Hà Thanh Special Forces Camp, Alpha Company recharged and refit–and prepared for further operations.

Looking back, Al Matheson said, "If [Lieutenant Enners] had not been there that day, I may be mistaken–I will never know–I believe I would have been choppered out of Hà Thanh the following day wrapped in a poncho, marked KIA."

Doc clearly recalled, "At first I didn't know who got killed. We got the wounded out, and then word came back that [Lieutenant] Enners, Maestas, and Kermit were killed. My heart almost stopped. The fire was so bad, we couldn't get the bodies out."

Several years after Ray's death, Captain Adams said, "The troops didn't want to accept Ray's death. Ray's passing had a significant effect on Alpha [Company]."

Four days after the harrowing firefight at Xã Ky Mao and severely under staffed, Alpha Company, acting as a relief force for the besieged SF Camp, engaged the NVA once again in the morning hours at Out Post #7. OPs 3, 4, and 7 came under rocket attack at 0440 hours. As they approached OP 7, Specialist Fourth Class McAlarney was shocked to see the NVA flag perched on top of the outpost. Under heavy fire, they succeeded in pushing the NVA off the hill and retook OP 7. Lieutenant Colonel Guinn's helicopter made a forced landing after incurring damage to the tail rotor section from an enemy RPG. Four Soldiers in his command section also suffered wounds.

Alpha Company pursued the enemy toward a fortified village south of the OP, engaging the NVA along the way and killing three. An unknown size force re-engaged Alpha Company from bunkers and tunnels that resulted in a two and one-half hour firefight. A sweep of the battleground afterwards confirmed ten

NVA KIA. McAlarney remembers pulling dead NVA soldiers from a bunker and finding an NVA officer alive hidden under the dead bodies.

As they swept east through a small group of huts, Alpha Company engaged the NVA once again, fighting from a series of bunkers and tunnels. In the skirmish, NVA losses amounted to fifteen KIA and one captured. The NVA suffered, as losses for the day totaled thirty-one. Thanks to Alpha Company's presence, the Special Forces Camp was once again under friendly control.

The third phase of *Tet* ended on 23 September 1968.

Operation Champaign Grove concluded at 2400 hours on 24 September 1968. During this campaign, a total of forty-one U.S. Soldiers were killed and 166 wounded. Of that, the 1st battalion 20th Infantry suffered eighteen killed and seventy wounded. Alpha Company lost eight KIHA. The enemy, both North Vietnamese and Việt Cộng, suffered 372 killed and two POWs taken. The 1-20th accounted for ninety-eight enemy killed.

During Operation Champaign Grove, Battalion Commander Lieutenant Colonel Guinn assessed the enemy in his AAR. "With a couple of exceptions the NVA did not actively seek contact with our forces. The NVA, however, were forced to fight, fought hard and well. Their defensive positions were exceptionally well prepared and indicated a trained and disciplined force. Their equipment was relatively new and appeared to be maintained properly."

He went on to say, "The success of this operation is attributed to the aggressive action by elements of this command [1-20th Infantry] and immediate response by Tac Air, Artillery, and Army aviation [gunships]."

Guinn added. "They would never stand and fight us. They would engage, break contact, and disappear. On this particular occasion [18 September 1968] when [Ray] was killed, they stayed, fought, and then broke contact. Brave and resourceful, when [Ray] went into that ambush, he was leading his men. They went into the jungle in perfect formation. He just walked into an ambush. The NVA were well camouflaged. You couldn't see them."

Normally the NVA would let one squad pass before they opened up, but because Matheson compromised their concealed position, the NVA engaged the second man in the file, Matheson. If the NVA waited, more men in 3rd platoon would have been wounded or killed.

Back home, as the draft calls increased, the dissent for the war amplified. Protests and anti-war cries gained traction and grew stronger. Draft dodging and desertion in all military services escalated, deserters fleeing to Canada, Mexico, or Sweden for safe haven. In FY 1968, deserters accounted for 2.9 percent of the armed forces.

Music of the late 1960s added to the fervor of discontent. Rock bands emphasized lyrics in their songs that overtly opposed the war and belittled the American Soldier. Joan Baez's "Saigon Bride" and the Doors's "The Unknown Soldier" energized and strengthened the protestors' cause. Whereas Barry Sadler's song in 1966, "Ballad of the Green Berets," paid tribute to the U.S. Army's most noted warriors, the 1968 song by The Byrds, "Draft Morning," twisted the very reason our Soldiers fought in Vietnam:

> Sun warm on my face, I hear you
> Down below movin' slow
> And it's morning
>
> Take my time this morning, no hurry
> To learn to kill and take the will
> From unknown faces
> Today was the day for action
> Leave my bed to kill instead
> Why should it happen?

On a broader scale, due to mounting pressure on Congress in Washington, Operation Rolling Thunder would end 31 October, and President Johnson would call for a halt of the bombing of North Vietnam.

By year-end 1968, U.S. forces reached 549,500 troops and 16,592 killed in hostile action. Congress and the American people strengthened their resolve that it was time to leave Vietnam.

As history would play out, America's military would never see victory in Vietnam, only firefights and battles that would seize some of America's best. In subsequent years, America would witness anguish and heartache for the physically and psychologically wounded. An aura of defeat would hover over America's military–flounder without a purpose trying to regain its footing and proud heritage.

Part III

"All Gave Some,
Some Gave All"

Chapter Twelve

COMING HOME

"It is foolish and wrong to mourn
the men who died. Rather we should
thank God that such men lived."

General George S. Patton, Jr.
USMA 1909

M y mother heard a *tap, tap, tap* on the front door.
It was the middle of the afternoon on 19 September, a beautiful fall day; white alto cumulous clouds randomly painted the bright blue sky. My father had already left the house to catch the Long Island Express train to New York City. Sandra was at school.

Since Ray's departure for Vietnam on 8 July my mother always wondered whether she would face the agony of a telegram or the visit of a military officer, what she was about to encounter. Every mother and father whose son or daughter goes off to war has nightmares wondering whether that day would arrive.

That day, in fact, had arrived.

She opened the door and stood rigid, paralyzed with fear. Her rapidly beating heart overcame her. Standing on the stoop was a non-commissioned officer and Lieutenant Michael Petrone in Class "A" Army greens, telegram in hand. Her face turned pale and her body trembled. Her worst nightmare rattled the calm of the day. While the trauma of it all caused her not to remember all that he said, she knew her son suffered the ultimate fate, death in combat.

He asked if she was Mrs. Enners. She said, "Yes." Lieutenant Petrone read the telegram.

The Secretary of the Army has asked me to express his regret that your son First Lieutenant Raymond J. Enners died in Vietnam on 18 September 1968 as a result of wounds received while on [a] combat operation when engaging a hostile force in a firefight. Please accept my deepest sympathy. Kenneth G. Widkham, Major General USA.

My mother broke into tears, the pain sickening and unspeakable. Lieutenant Petrone went on to say, "I am very sorry for your loss." He handed the telegram to my mom. As Mom's memories of Ray flashed before her eyes, the pain intensified.

How did it happen and why Ray she asked. Lieutenant Petrone had no specific information at the time. Ray was only twenty-two years old, nearing his twenty-third birthday.

It takes a special person to notify parents of a Soldier's death. To walk to the front door, knock, and deliver that awful news with honor and dignity takes special courage. Lieutenant Petrone did not know Ray or my parents. It was as difficult for him to bring such horrible news as it was for my mom to hear it. He did the very best he could. By the end of 1968, Soldiers like Lieutenant Petrone would deliver death notifications to more than 16,500 families.

Mom called my dad at work and could hardly get the words out of her mouth. She had no details to share. She just wanted him home. For Dad, it was a long and painful one hour ride home on the train. His memories of Ray growing up were vivid—fishing in the Long Island Sound, attending New York Yankee baseball and Giants football games. Sandra recalled the day she found out about Ray.

> Many say our childhood was idyllic—good strong family values, lots of open space to grow, extended family within a few mile radius, roots that tied us to our community that reached back generations— but the day I bounced off the school bus from field hockey practice met by my tearful father at the door, my life was forever changed. I learned at an early age just how fragile life can be and the long reaching effects that last a lifetime. I had never seen my father cry.

That same day upon hearing the news, Betty Adams, stricken with grief, immediately drove to the north athletic field at West Point where we were practicing off-season lacrosse. She broke the news to Coach Adams. "That was very tough to take," said Adams. He was devastated but at that moment did not inform me of the tragedy.

That afternoon, the letter Ray wrote on the 13th arrived home. That compounded Mom's despondent emotional state.

Shortly after dinner at the cadet mess hall, the 3rd Regimental Commander on the Commandant's staff, Colonel R. Maladowitz, visited my room. As roommate and lacrosse teammate Tom Cafaro was in the room with me that evening, Colonel Maladowitz asked if we could be alone. He advised me that Ray died in combat, that he made the ultimate sacrifice. I was shocked and had so many questions, but understandably, so few answers were available, the details not yet available.

He suggested that I wait to go home until my brother's body arrived, but I remember saying, "I'd like to talk to my parents about it tonight." I did, and they wanted me to be at home with them and my sister. I departed the next day.

In these situations, I learned to take one day at a time. It can be overwhelming to lose a family member, particularly in combat. I thought about all that he was, all that he accomplished, and all that he trained for–I thought about the honor of it all.

I understood the dangers of combat. I understood Ray volunteered to serve in Vietnam. At the same time, I questioned whether our country expects too much of its youth, too much from its Soldiers.

Over time, I resolved in my mind that he served for a just cause; that he, as many Soldiers did, served his country with pride. Fortunately, for most, they returned home alive, but for others, they did not. Over 58,000 men and women who served in Vietnam returned home in a flag draped casket.

In the days that followed, my parents had many visitors and phone calls, family, friends, and classmates asking how they could help ease the pain. I remember everyone being kind and caring. They brought food for lunch and dinner. A torrent of condolences and praise for Ray followed, for several months. My parents received so many letters from Soldiers Ray served with, teachers from high school, coaches, cadets, Chaplain James David Ford and Assistant Chaplain Wilson at West Point, and Ray's classmates.

I returned to West Point on the 22nd. As difficult as it was to focus on academics for the next few days, I did. Several classmates and roommate Tom Cafaro eased the pain of Ray's death. Chaplins Ford and Wilson asked me to visit them in their office on the 23rd. In a calming tone, they told me how much they respected Ray. He served as an acolyte in the Protestant Chapel for the four years he attended West Point. We talked and their words had a relaxing effect. I did not attend off-season lacrosse practice for the next two days. My head just was not in the game.

"We resumed school work," said Sandra. "And then the reality of his death hit us head on once again." Ray's body arrived home on the 26th.

I returned home on the twenty-seventh. On Saturday the twenty-eighth, Ray lay in his coffin at the Arthur White Funeral Home in Farmingdale. "Having no experience with the loss of a loved one, I was paralyzed with fear to enter the funeral parlor and couldn't go in until my brother [Rich] all but dragged me in", said Sandra. Friends, family, acquaintances, and newspaper reporters flooded the funeral home. Tears flowed, memories of Ray awakened from their dormant state, and one by one with heads bowed visitors paid their respects to Ray.

The casket was open. Ray was at peace.

Religious services were held on Sunday, the 29th, at St. Luke's Lutheran Church in Farmingdale, the small church we belonged to on Main Street. Ray, Sandra, and I attended Sunday school and church there, and Ray and I served as acolytes. Reverend James R. Corgee delivered the sermon and eulogy. Several comments he made resonated with me at the time, one in particular. He said, "Ray never asked questions of what his duties were. He never complained. He knew his responsibilities. He did what he had to do and did it with excellence."

Sandra remembered, "The funeral service was surreal, something I will never forget. The church was overflowing to the outside, an outpouring of love and grief and respect, and people singing the hymn 'Onward Christian Soldiers' could be heard loudly."

Pastor Corgee's final words were, "We all shall see him again."

A very solemn service it was, and the surge of relatives and friends was overwhelming. Emotions were rampant, and for some, the pain intolerable.

The burial was set for 2:30 p.m. Monday 30 September at the West Point Cemetery.

As I recall, it was a long journey to West Point, especially that day. My parents, sister, and I had made the trip many times before to visit my brother or to watch Ray and I play lacrosse. It was a straight forward trip, maybe sixty miles; west on the Long Island Expressway, across the George Washington Bridge, north on the Palisades Interstate Parkway to the Bear Mountain Bridge, and north on Route 9W through Fort Montgomery and the small town of Highland Falls, just outside the main gate of West Point.

Not that there were many miles to travel, but the death of our brother, the death of my parents' son, weighed heavy on us all. I could not fathom the pain that Mom and Dad felt deep in their hearts. There was no script to follow to ease the pain, no screenplay to mask our emotions. It would take time.

The procession entered through the main gate on Thayer Road as Ray and I had done many times before. I gazed to the right as we passed The Thayer Hotel. We rounded the bend near Trophy Point, and as we approached the cemetery, tears rolled down Mom's cheeks. She was proud of Ray, and I sensed her thoughts were random at best. Why did this have to happen? What really happened that day in September? Did he die because we raised him to be selfless in times of need?

As time went on, she would surely find out. We would all find out. Dad kept his emotions inside, but I know he was hurting. He had to be strong for the family. He comforted Mom. The air was cool and crisp with a gentle north breeze blowing off the Hudson River. The leaves on the trees were beginning their annual turn from green to a myriad of colors. Subtle hints of yellow, orange, and rust spotted the valley, a beautiful, uplifting sight, but a sharp contrast to the solemn emotions that permeated the day.

As we entered the West Point Cemetery, one could not help but feel the solitude and reverence to those interred. We first came upon the neo-classical designed Old Cadet Chapel, originally erected in 1836 and relocated to the cemetery, stone by stone, in 1910. Soldiers lie side by side, some since the Revolutionary War. They comfort each other; some knowing they died for a cause greater than themselves, others knowing that, over their careers, they served their nation proudly.

Many visitors gathered on the grounds at grave number 73, Row B of section XXXIV, just a stone's throw from several of his classmates who suffered the same fate as Ray in Southeast Asia. Friends from Ray's high school Class of '63 attended the burial, as did his and my classmates from West Point, cadets from Company B-1, Sandra's high school friends as well as my friends from Half Hollow Hills, family, and relatives. Lieutenant Chris Pettit, classmate, teammate, and friend, was able to get leave from his assignment in Germany to attend the funeral along with his wife Mary Anne.

Dad, Mom, Sandra, and I took our places, I sitting next to my mom. Others circled the burial site.

Burial was with full military honors. The Honor Guard consisted of classmates stationed nearby and members of the Class of '69 who were under Ray's command in Cadet Company B-1.

Chaplain Ford said a prayer and read verses from the Bible. My memory falters as to which ones.

A three-volley firing of rifles broke the silence of the solemn occasion.

As the Hell Cat bugler played taps, the somber tradition that signifies the extinguishing of life, a phrase from West Point's Alma Mater written by P.S. Reinecke in 1911, invaded my thoughts.

> And when our work is done,
> Our course on earth is run,
> May it be said, "Well done.
> Be thou at peace."

The Honor Guard folded the American flag that draped the casket thirteen times and with the utmost respect presented it to my mother, a very moving and meaningful event. The senior member of the Honor Guard said, "On behalf of the President of the United States, the United States Army, and a grateful Nation, please accept this flag as a symbol of our appreciation for your loved one's honorable and faithful service."

The ceremony jolted everyone in attendance. For this was the consequence of war, the discerning notion and realization that sometimes the burden of freedom bears human sacrifice. Holding my emotions inside was challenging, but I did.

As the senior member of the Honor Guard handed the triangular star-studded flag to Mom, I said, "His name will never die." Little did I know the impact of what I said. As the future unfolded, truer words were never spoke. Permanent remembrances of all kinds would follow. I did not return home at the conclusion of the burial. I returned to my studies, as difficult as that was.

Ray was finally at peace.

News spread quickly of Ray's death. It was not but four days after the burial, *Newsday*, *The Farmingdale Post*, and *The Long Island Press* wrote articles about Ray. In one article journalist Charles Clark said, "The war in Vietnam has claimed the life of one of the finest athletes ever produced in Suffolk County. Enners was a standout athlete at Half Hollow Hills High and at West Point."

Mike Lee, journalist from the *Long Island Press*, in a 3 November 1968 column wrote, "There is no complete way I can express Ray's true characteristics. It is refreshing to know that men like Ray are around to serve our country. To all who knew Ray, the fact that he would sacrifice his life for others is no surprise. He died as he lived—in an outstanding manner."

For the next several months, I visited the cemetery after dinner *every* evening; rain, sleet, or snow did not deter my walk to Ray's grave. It was my way of saluting a fallen hero, honoring my brother and paying tribute to a great American. Shoulder-to-shoulder Ray lay in the comfort of his classmates, Brothers in Arms, and historic military leaders that shaped America's course to freedom and a democratic way of life.

The Class of 1967 paid dearly for their service to country, their call to duty. While serving in war-torn South Vietnam, twenty-nine graduates of the class paid the ultimate price by giving their life to a noble cause.

On my visits to the cemetery, I gazed with curiosity at the gravestones and names of those interred. During my courses on military history, I studied generals like Major General John Buford, Union Cavalry Commander who was instrumental in the defeat of the Confederates at the Battle of Gettysburg. On one visit, I passed the grave of Brigadier General Sylvanus Thayer, father of the military academy. The impact of walking by their graves made what I had learned of these men and their feats of accomplishment even more real, more tangible. I could sense the fulfillment of life from those interred. I could sense the peace and serenity of the setting high above the winding Hudson River.

At other times, remembrances of Ray occupied my mind as I walked the cemetery grounds.

Fall turned to winter; snow covered the stark lonely site of his grave. A headstone was now in place. Winter turned to spring; trees were in bloom and birds nesting. Grass began to grow on the once barren dirt that covered his grave. With the passing of each month, additional classmates found their final resting place next to Ray due to the ravages of war.

My parents and sister continued to carry the burden of losing a son, a brother, trying to place his death in perspective. I struggled with my feelings. I wondered how we would fill that void. Ray and my family would have wanted me to press on, to continue playing lacrosse, to graduate, to be a Soldier and to serve the nation. I did just that. I always felt Ray's presence. Not a day went by that I did not think of him. He inspired me to confront new challenges, accomplish any mission, and win in a sportsmanlike way. Although nothing would fill the void, a bridge would have to do; a bridge that would link fond memories of his life with inspiration to confront any future challenge. He gave me strength and courage.

Sandra was sixteen, a junior in high school, and experienced the immeasurable pain that Mom and Dad were feeling. She experienced the wealth of support from friends, family, church, high school, and Ray's classmates that enabled Mom and Dad to function in their daily lives. Sandra said, "Rich, a cadet at

West Point, gave my parents reason to stay involved with West Point, Army lacrosse, and an opportunity to visit Ray's grave, all serving to ease their pain."

She recalled the dynamics of living at home:

> During the day and in public we all carried on, but at night or home alone, the loss and accompanying grief and sadness would creep in for each of us in different ways. As time went on, the awards and accolades honoring the memory of Ray would be a great comfort to us all.

> In retrospect, I can say it was Ray's calling to be a soldier. I remember overhearing family, parishioners, and friends commenting on how he carried the cross in processions before the church service when he served as an acolyte in his teens. His posture was amazingly straight, strong as though he was already a soldier marching.

> Ray was born when our father was oversees in World War II. Dad knew what it meant to be a soldier in combat. The last thing he said to Ray before he [Ray] left was "Keep your head down, 'ya hear." Later, in his grief, he would blame himself, regretting he did not say more in an effort to protect him. I overheard my dad say to my mom, "I should have said to him 'Don't be a hero.'" Even though the official diagnosis was heart disease, I always believed my father died twelve years later at the age of sixty-one from a "broken heart."

> Mother soldiered on joining the American Gold Star Mothers, a support group of mothers who had lost their sons in war, and found a full time job to get out of the house and keep her mind occupied. When I had a son of my own, I could not imagine surviving the loss of a child. I asked mom how she could go on. She said, "You find a way to live with it, but you never forget."

> The war in Vietnam raged on, and the protests against the war at home reached epic proportions among college and high school students in 1969. My parents, always patriotic, believed in our country, the war, and [never allowed] any discussion to the contrary. In my adolescent world where everyone wants to fit in,

I was pressured to protest the war. While I hated the war because it took my beloved brother, I silently straddled both sides, not wanting to antagonize anyone. I suffered a great deal of internal conflict.

The loss of their first-born son would take a toll on my parents, as hard as they tried. Experienced by any parent who buries their child, a piece of their hearts and spirits were forever broken. My once happy, carefree home life always had an underlying sadness, a trauma that would always be with us. In a sense, I not only lost my brother, but my family and the inherent security adolescents thrive on. I found myself seeking the comfort of friends' homes more often and trying to "fix things" at home, trying to bring joy back, but, of course, I could not repair the wound that would always be there. I would continue in that direction in my adult life.

"Al Matheson was in the hospital when Chris and I went to visit [his] parents," said Mary Anne Pettit. Chris was struggling with Ray's death–how it happened and why occupied his mind on a daily basis. He thought talking with Al's parents would somehow ease the pain. "I can see it; we sat in their den. It was difficult for the parents to talk as Chris was sobbing." Chris wanted to hear the story over and over again, trying desperately to make sense of it all.

Chris felt a bond, a type of connection with Al's parents. "It was very profound," said Mary Anne. "The day that we spent with the Mathesons left an indelible mark on my heart. Chris didn't only consider Ray a friend; he was like a brother. On occasion Chris would read books by Aristotle on friendship, trying to make sense of the loss."

Ed Sullivan reflected back on the many stories that involved him and Ray. "It was a friendship cut short by his death," said Ed. "His death made combat more personal for me, more serious. It certainly impressed upon me that life is precious. You need to value every minute."

Dad and Mom visited West Point during the winter months in early 1969, weather permitting, and more frequently in the spring to see my lacrosse games. They loved the sport. Under Coach Adams, it was a good year for Army lacrosse. We won ten games and lost only one. The most notable was a win over Navy

14-4 on their home turf at Marine Corps Memorial Stadium. That year we shared the NCAA National Championship with Johns Hopkins.

On every visit, they paid their respects to Ray at the cemetery. It comforted them. To maintain that parent to son connection was so important. Lacrosse season finished at the end of May, and it would not be until "June Week" 7 June 1969 that Mom, Dad, and Sandra would return to West Point for the presentation of the Distinguished Service Cross by Superintendent Major General Samuel W. Koster. At the ceremony, Major General Koster made poignant remarks about Ray's dedication to Duty, Honor, Country. He praised Ray for his sacrifice and selfless service to the nation. As he did, memories of Ray flashed before my eyes—fishing in Lake Winnipesaukee, Ray teaching me how to kick extra points, and water skiing on Long Island Sound. Tears filled Mom's, Dad's, and Sandra's eyes. It was a warm, heartfelt, but emotional ceremony.

The military awards presented at West Point were only the beginning of the honors, accolades, and remembrances bestowed upon Ray after his death. They would include athletic awards, a college scholarship fund, and honors that would carry his name, honors that represented and symbolized his character, courage, and leadership.

Chapter Thirteen

REMEMBERING RAY

"A nation reveals itself not only by the men it produces,
but also by the men it honors;
the men it remembers."

John F. Kennedy, 1963

F ew Americans speak of the Vietnam War. It receded from the headlines many years ago. Like a bruise that never healed, the war left an indelible mark on many. There are those who abhorred the war; in fact, they abhor any war. There are those that were just apathetic. There are those who supported the war, but wrestled with the misalignment of government policy and military objectives. Most Soldiers in the military did not overtly voice their opinions. That was not a luxury. They just did their job.

More than 2.7 million Soldiers served in Vietnam, some 300,000 wounded and more than 58,200 men and women killed serving their country in the most traumatic and unpopular war of modern times. The war has long been over, but the vivid recollections never cease in the minds of many. For those that returned home alive, some talk about their service. Many choose to forget, for the pain is too much to bear. Some still carry the burden and guilt of the death of a comrade and ask *why not me*. They carry the invisible scars and graphic images of the destruction of human life and property that was so prevalent. Their healing continues, thanks in part to the many memorials that honor the Vietnam Veterans, one in particular, the Vietnam Veterans Memorial in Washington, D.C.

The Wall was the idea of one man, Jan C. Scruggs, a combat Veteran. Conceived as much for the living as for the dead, The Wall welcomes home the living and pays homage to the departed. It is an emotional and stimulating reminder of the many Soldiers that served and died when duty called. Scruggs along with Jack Wheeler (USMA 1966), Bob Doubek and other Veteran officers and enlisted personnel put America on a path to healing with their innovative ideas, drive and pursuit of reconciliation.

As you gaze upon the Wall from a distance, it seems simple, unassuming, a portrait of stonework emerging from the earth. As you approach the Wall and descend the walkway, you are overwhelmed with a feeling of sorrow and reverence. Your attention traverses to the upwardly sloping highly polished black granite, the reflection of which reveals the living. For Veterans that approach the Wall, the reflection speaks. It says you served your country honorably. For the parents of the fallen, the reflection says you raised a son or daughter who proudly embraced American ideals. For visitors, the Wall screams, *we answered the call of duty.*

You walk further. You realize the names of those who gave their lives are etched deeply into the purity of the glistening stone according to the date they fell. Their voices now silent but the mystique of the memorial speaks volumes. Their names represent faces of those who made the ultimate sacrifice–some experiencing pain–but all demonstrating commitment, courage, and service to country. They are sons, daughters, husbands, brothers, sisters, friends, and classmates.

The names inscribed on the wall have a magnetic like pull that draws you closer. You contemplate that they gave their lives for a nation that wanted to forget; Vietnam was a war that America did not win. It was a war of battles and politics. It was a war that tore the nation apart and a war that splintered the military.

In November 1992 on the tenth anniversary of the memorial, General Michael S. Davison, USA (Ret.) said, "The polished black stone [on the Wall] not only reflects the respectful visitors who pass in front of it but also reaches out to bring into its reflection the trees and clouds and the sky. Thus, it surrounds the names of those who gave their lives with nature's tribute as well as the tribute of those who come to honor the departed heroes." On that same momentous occasion out of deep respect for Ray, Ed Sullivan read Ray's name as was done by others for all 58,200 names. Ed said, "This [was] one of the most meaningful things I have done in my life. Ray did a lot for me, and the way he led and lived his life still adds meaning to mine."

In combat, there is valor. In valor, there is a hint of hope, hope that a Soldier's death is not in vain and hope that a Soldier's sacrifice and service to the nation are never forgotten. Those who served and those who gave their lives did not ask for praise, nor did they ask for medals. They only asked that we remember their service and devotion to duty.

Many have honored Ray in other humbling ways, ways not sculpted in bronze, not carved in marble or granite. Tributes emerged untethered by time, thanks to a grateful nation, Brothers in Arms, classmates of the Long Gray Line, coaches, and scholars. Teammate Chris Pettit once wrote, "I have come to believe that [Ray] lives on in many people's memories and wherever lacrosse is played."

I present these awards and accolades on behalf of a grateful Enners family.

The Distinguished Service Cross

The nation's second highest award for valor, the Distinguished Service Cross was established by an act of Congress (65th Congress) on 2 January 1918 under President Woodrow Wilson and given for extraordinary heroism in connection with hostile action with an enemy of the United States. Ray's citation from the Department of the Army General Orders 403 reads as follows:

> For extraordinary heroism in connection with military operations involving conflict with an armed hostile force in the Republic of Vietnam, First Lieutenant Enners distinguished himself by exceptionally valorous actions on 18 September 1968 while serving as a platoon leader during a combat sweep near the village of Hà Thanh.

> While moving across a small valley, his platoon was ambushed by a reinforced North Vietnamese Army squad firing machine guns, automatic weapons and small arms from camouflaged positions on a hillside. A squad leader was severely wounded and fell within twenty meters of the communists. Helplessly trapped by raking fire from the enemy gunners, the badly bleeding squad leader called for help, but the deadly hostile fire kept anyone from reaching him. Lieutenant Enners, hearing his cries, began moving forward to rescue him. From his position one hundred meters back, he crawled forward through the rice paddies and leaped across the intervening dikes, dodging through continuous bursts of enemy fire until he reached his forward squad trapped behind a dike twenty meters from the fallen squad leader.

> With the aid of one of the other squad leaders, he dispersed his men and signaled for covering fire. He and the squad leader then jumped

over the dike and ran forward through the blistering fire to within ten meters of the wounded man, but were forced to turn back when the North Vietnamese began throwing grenades. Calling for a second burst of covering fire, the two men again raced across the bullet-ridden paddies, only to be halted again by the shrapnel of exploding grenades.

Returning to the scant cover of the dike, Lieutenant Enners reorganized his men, maneuvering one squad twenty meters to the right of the enemy emplacements and directing the remainder of the platoon to areas from which they could lay down the most effective cross fire. Signaling a third time for his men to open up on the aggressors, he and the squad leader vaulted the dike and again attempted to reach the wounded man. Braving the rounds scorching the air around them, they raced to the injured man's position and took cover behind the dike. After applying first aid to the man's wounds while the squad leader fired at the North Vietnamese, Lieutenant Enners picked up the injured man and again disregarding the risk to his own life carried him back across the battlefield to the care of medical aidmen.

Moving to the squad on the right flank, he then led an attack on the communists. Charging through a hail of fire, he moved to within fifteen meters of the enemy before he was fatally wounded by hostile machine gun fire. First Lieutenant Enners' extraordinary heroism and devotion to duty, at the cost of his life, were in keeping with the highest traditions of the military service and reflect great credit upon himself, his unit, and the United States Army.

The Bronze Star Medal

Established 4 February 1944, the Bronze Star Medal is awarded for meritorious achievement in ground operations against hostile forces.

The Purple Heart

Formerly known as The Badge of Military Merit, General Douglas MacArthur on 22 February 1932, the 200th anniversary of George Washington's birthday, revived the Purple Heart. The Armed Forces of the United States award this medal to Soldiers wounded or killed in hostile action by an enemy of the United States.

National Order of Vietnam Fifth Class

Per their decree dated 15 August 1950, the Government of the Republic of Vietnam gave this award to:

> Servicemen of courage and rare self-sacrifice, they displayed at all times the most tactful cooperation while aiding the Armed Forces of the Republic of Vietnam to repel the Red wave undermining South Vietnam and Southeast Asia. With ready zeal and commendable response, they fought on to the end in every mission and set a brilliant example for their fellow soldiers. They died in the performance of their duty. Behind them they leave the abiding grief of their former comrades-in-arms, Vietnamese as well as American.

The Vietnam Gallantry Cross with Palm

The award with palm was the highest in its class and given by the Government of the Republic of Vietnam per their decree dated 15 August 1950. The South Vietnamese Government awarded this citation to service members for:

> Accomplishing deeds of valor or displaying heroic conduct while fighting the enemy.

Foley · Enners · Nathe Lacrosse Center

Currently under construction at the northeast corner of Michie Stadium, this building will house West Point's lacrosse office, locker room, and training center for both men and women. It will "provide our cadet-athletes, coaches, and alumni with a first-class facility that represents our commitment to the program now and into the future," said Boo Corrigan, Director of Athletics. Classmate Bill Foley pledged the lead gift to make this happen. Classmate Mike Nathe also gave his life in Vietnam. USMA Superintendent Lieutenant General Robert L. Caslen, Class of '75, said of Ray and Mike, "Raymond and Mike took the mental, physical, and leadership skills they developed as lacrosse players to the fight in Vietnam where they gave their last full measure of their devotion. Because of Bill's respect and love of his classmates, this facility will forever honor them and their memory."

Ray Enners Wing at the Kimsey Athletic Center

Larry Izzo, classmate and Brother in Arms, through his gift to West Point was instrumental in naming a hallway in the Kimsey Athletic Center in Ray's honor. In August 2003 at the dedication ceremony, Larry Izzo gave a heartfelt and heartwarming speech about his and Ray's friendship, as did other classmates about theirs with Ray. After the 150-pound football season, having never played lacrosse, Ray convinced Larry to try out for off-season lacrosse. "In typical unselfish fashion, Ray spent hours and hours teaching me how to pass and catch," said Larry. "I was indebted to Ray for life." Larry played lacrosse for Army all four years. Having battled pancreatic cancer for several years, he passed away in October 2003.

First LT. Raymond J. Enners Award

This annual award some call the "Heisman Trophy" of lacrosse and first awarded in 1969 is given by the United States Intercollegiate Lacrosse Association (USILA) to The Outstanding Collegiate Lacrosse Player in the nation in men's Division I lacrosse. The two individuals that cultivated the interest with the USILA were classmate, teammate, and two-time first team All-American Chris Pettit and Coach Jim "Ace" Adams.

Tom Cafaro, winner of the Jack Turnbull Award in 1971 for the best attackman in the nation, two-time first team All-American at Army, inductee into the National Lacrosse Hall of Fame in 1988, and inductee into the Army Sports Hall of Fame in 2007, said this about the Enners Award he received in 1971:

> Rich and I were roommates when Ray died. It was my first personal experience with battlefield death, and seeing the anguish of Rich and his family had a profound impact on me.

I knew I had a chance at the best player award named for Ray, and somewhere along the line, it became important to me to win it. In some way, I felt as if it would be keeping it in the family.

After graduation, I became Ray's surrogate as best man at Rich's wedding and godfather to his oldest son Sean. When Sean was born, I knew immediately that the award would go to him when he was old enough. It is a wonderful reminder of an amazing man and uncle he never got to meet and the selfless courage Ray displayed saving the life of a soldier and forfeiting his own life as he tried to save another.

Doug Schreiber from Half Hollow Hill High School, winner of the LT. Donald C. McLaughlin Memorial Trophy for the best midfielder in the nation in 1973, two-time All-American at the University of Maryland, and inductee into the Lacrosse Hall of Fame in 1993, recalled his memories of Ray and his receiving the Enners Award in 1973:

Growing up and attending Half Hollow Hills schools, I soon became aware of the name Ray Enners. After I watched Ray play football, basketball, and lacrosse, he became my idol, my hero.

Watching Ray play sports was special; great athlete, tough competitor, humble, and respected by all. I wanted to be a great player like Ray.

I remember the sad day in 1968, hearing about Ray's death. My family and I attended his wake, a tremendous outpouring of love and respect. As in life a hero, as in death a hero, not only a great athlete, a great son and brother, teammate and soldier. He died a hero.

Not long after, I was having a catch with my brother Ed, who was playing at Cortland [State] at the time, in our backyard, when he said if I kept working hard and put the extra time in, one day I could win the Ray Enners Award and win a national championship. From that time forward, I dedicated myself to achieve these goals. I was highly motivated and determined to one day receive an award named after my hero, Ray Enners #26. Ray was unique, a great athlete, great leader, on and off the field, very humble, a man of high character.

Ray wore #26 throughout his career. After graduating high school, I switched my jersey number to #26 in honor of Ray. I wore #26 at Nassau Community College and later at the University of Maryland. I shared the Ray Enners story with my children, who both attended St. Anthony's High School and played lacrosse. They both wore #26.

Today my daughter plays lacrosse at Rutgers University, wearing #26. When my son arrived at Princeton, #26 was not available, but after graduating and now playing professionally for the Ohio Machine in the Major Lacrosse League, he wears #26.

Winning the Ray Enners Award in 1973 was the highlight of my athletic career. His life and story inspired me; it drove me to be the best I could be. Having known Ray and his family, the award was especially meaningful. It is not often that a person like Ray comes along, I truly feel honored to have known Ray and his family.

A week prior to winning the Ray Enners Award, my college team won the national championship. Without question, the Ray Enners Award was my proudest moment. I will never forget that night. The award had a positive effect on my life.

Ray's story is that of true hero; his story has inspired so many. I am very grateful to the Enners family.

NCAA All-American Lacrosse Honors

Ray was an honorable mention pick at the United States Military Academy at West Point in 1967. First awarded in 1922, the USILA annually picks the top athletes in the sport for the positions of Attack, Midfielder, Defense, and Goalie. Selections are made for first, second, third teams, and honorable mention for Division I, Division II, and Division III.

Long Island Metropolitan Lacrosse Foundation Hall of Fame

The Long Island Metropolitan Lacrosse Foundation (LIMLF), established in 1985, incorporated a charter to "protect and extend the heritage of lacrosse on Long Island and honor those individuals who have been most important in the development and continuity of this wonderful game." The LIMLF board nominates and the membership votes on prospective candidates. LIMLF inducted Ray into the Hall of Fame in 2004. The citation read, "Raymond established an outstanding record of excellence throughout his athletic career, and demonstrated a dedicated commitment to the great sport of Lacrosse on Long Island that warrants attention and gratitude."

Suffolk County Sports Hall of Fame

Established in 1990, the Suffolk County Sports Hall of Fame honors outstanding persons, living or deceased, who have gained prominence and have made substantial contributions on behalf of themselves and Suffolk County, in the fields of all professional and amateur sports. SCSHF inducted Ray into the Hall of Fame in 1991. On the concourse wall at the Long Island MacArthur Airport is a picture of Ray among the likes of Boomer Esiason and Carl Yastrzemski.

LT. Raymond Enners Award

First awarded in 1970, the Suffolk County Boys Lacrosse Coaches Association gives this award annually to the top lacrosse player in Suffolk County, Long Island, who best exemplifies courage, teamwork, skill, and leadership. Kieran Mullins, the 2014 winner of the award, said:

> Upon receiving the LT. Raymond Enners Award, I was truly humbled to be associated with such a decorated soldier and athlete. Although I have obviously never met LT. Enners, I feel as if I know him, and we would have been great friends. We share the Brotherhood of lacrosse, playing for West Point, and being soldiers. We also had the remarkable opportunity to share each of these experiences with our own blood brothers, Rich Enners

and my brother Shea. LT. Enners excelled because he made those around him better on the lacrosse field and off. As my role model, this is the code by which I hope to live my life as a player and a person.

Kieran Mullins' coach Keith Scheidel of Islip High School said:

> When someone wins the Ray Enners award, you know they are the best of the best. After Kieran Mullins received this award, the hardest challenge I had was writing his speech. I wanted to give Kieran the acknowledgement that he deserved. After doing research on Ray, I know he deserved as much credit as Kieran did on that night. The more research I did, the more I felt like Kieran was able to keep the Ray Enners name alive. They had so many things in common. He is by far the most unselfish player I have ever coached. His priority was always to help his team win. It was never about individual performance. His character is based on kindness, unselfishness, integrity, discipline, and respect.

> After speaking with Kieran, he is going to try to wear Ray's number [26] at West Point. It was a great moment for Kieran and Islip Lacrosse. We could not be more proud to have an Islip Lacrosse player win this award.

All-Suffolk County and All-Long Island Lacrosse Team

Ray was voted as a first team pick in 1963 by coaches for the position of Attack. These are the best players in Suffolk Country and Long Island in their respective positions. With sixty-eight chapters in forty-five states, U.S. Lacrosse is the governing body that establishes rules and regulations for the selection process.

Long Island Press Athlete-Scholar Award

High school guidance counselors and coaches nominate students for this annual award. The *Long Island Press* presented this award to Ray in 1963 based on his leadership ability, athletic skills, grade point average, and what he contributed to the school and community.

LT. Ray Enners-Chris Pettit Award

Teammate Chris Pettit initially established this award in Ray's name in 1969, and I subsequently added Chris's name to the award after his death in 1997. Given annually, it honors West Point's Most Valuable Offensive Player in lacrosse.

Raymond J. Enners Memorial Fund

Established in 1969 by classmate Chris Pettit and the Half Hollow Hills High School district, this award assists young men through college financially who best exemplify the attributes of Ray. Former Athletic Director Anne Dignam said, "It is given to the athlete-scholar who exhibits the character and talent of Enners. The award is not presented every year. It is very selective, only when we have a candidate that has the same qualities and characteristics that Ray had."

The honors received and memorials bestowed upon Ray over the years have been humbling, to say the least. He lived his life thinking of others, and we can only hope that the memory of who he was and what he accomplished will continue to inspire others in a positive way.

Fortunately, hope will survive the passage of time.

Chapter Fourteen

A PERSPECTIVE

"Leadership is a potent combination of
strategy and character.
But if you must be without one,
be without strategy."

General Norman Schwarzkopf
USMA 1956

While attending West Point, I knew little of combat, only its historical significance and consequences. When I graduated, President Nixon was bringing the troops home. Had I been asked to serve in Vietnam, I would have faithfully done so. By the end of 1971, the number of Soldiers in Vietnam dwindled to less than 157,000. It was a slow and agonizing withdrawal; a progression of defeat that caused the nation to question its policy of fighting wars on foreign soil. Not having served in Southeast Asia, I could only visualize the feats of heroism of many Soldiers and the challenges of soldiering in that environment.

What I do know, however, is what it is like to lose a brother and how the loss of Ray affected our family. Throughout my life, I never lost sight of my brother's accomplishments, perhaps partly because there were several reminders. The honors and awards were an "aide-mémoire" of his life and hints to live life embracing a firm set of beliefs.

What gives me some consolation for his death are the lessons learned from his actions both on and off the battlefield. The combination of character, competence, and mission orientation played a significant role in determining his actions in combat as they did in other facets of his life. It began with a belief system founded in values derived from our parents, his teachers, and his coaches, whom he universally respected. Integrity, respect for others, accountability, the importance of working as a team, humility, and hard work epitomized Ray's moral fiber throughout his life. It formed the basis of his leadership style and characterized the decisions he made.

The knowledge gained at West Point and its culture of Duty, Honor, Country broadened and strengthened his belief system and gave him skills necessary to lead under any set of circumstances. He placed the needs of the nation, the U.S. Army, and subordinates above his own. Former President Ronald Reagan brought to light the impact of West Point on its graduates in a statement made on 28 October 1987. For "more than 180 years West Point in this time has established and added luster to a proud story, a story of courage and wisdom, a story of heroism, of sacrifice, and yes, very often the ultimate sacrifice."

More advanced technical and tactical knowledge came from Ray's experiences afterwards, at IOBC, Ranger School, and his brief assignment at Fort Carson, Colorado. That, I believe, boosted his confidence and enabled him to act in a particular way when faced with the heightened threat of danger in combat. These factors combined, plus pure desire, drove him to lead from the front, to lead by example, to lead with strength and optimism.

The U.S. Army has a doctrine that extends to all who join its ranks - officers, non-commissioned officers, and enlisted personnel alike. It requires and expects a Soldier to live to a higher standard, demonstrating at all times loyalty, duty, respect, selfless service, honor, integrity, and personal courage. Dr. Michael D. Matthews, Professor of Engineering Psychology at West Point, said, "The military socializes (trains) soldiers to put the team above the self. This probably doesn't 'take' in everyone, all the time, but this socialization process increases the odds that at least some soldiers will make heroic actions in disregard for their own safety."

Ray's psychological makeup contributed to defining his leadership style. Effective leaders set standards, and standards determine the worth of a leader. My brother set high standards, always did. He continuously pushed himself a little further, raised the hurdle a little higher. As evidence of his nickname in high school, Mr. Machine, he pushed others as well to maximize their potential but only after setting a higher personal level of performance. Yes, his drive was to increase his own effectiveness as a leader, but the effects of this instilled a level of commitment and motivation in others. He led teammates and subordinates, not through position or rank, but influence. The example he set encouraged others to do things because they wanted to.

It is a challenge to place into words what it means to be selfless, but the West Point Prayer sheds light on this. "Encourage us in our endeavor to live above the common level of life. Make us to choose the harder right instead of the easier wrong." Some might say selflessness is a virtue. Some might say it is a leadership trait. Yet, some might call it an aspiration. However one defines it, selflessness, whether displayed on the battlefield or elsewhere, is descriptive of a deed performed by an individual who lives "above the common level of life."

I can only surmise combat releases different types of fundamental truths, hope or despair, courage or self-preservation, empathy or tough love, humbleness or self-gratification, life or death. For a platoon leader, events move quickly on the battlefield, and one must adapt sound reasoning for actions taken during the myriad of complex and changing situations. You have split seconds to think and act. I understand the pressure is immeasurable.

Those who have served as platoon leaders in combat (or other leadership roles) told me it is a very challenging position that carries complex burdens, the most important of which is accountability, accountability for the mission, and in the context of the mission, the responsibility of those in your command. There are no excuses for not completing a mission. There is no one to blame but the one in charge. "Mentally, he must carry the burden of responsibility for all his soldiers all the time," said Glynn. "He must remain focused, alert, and decisive as horrendous things are occurring around him. He must save his mourning for another time. Soldiers always watch their leaders, but never more intently than when the proverbial 'shit hits the fan.'"

What was going on in Ray's mind during the brutal firefight of 18 September near Hà Thanh we will never know, but perhaps his actions speak for his state of mind. Combat is a delicate balance between accomplishing the mission and protecting the Soldiers in one's command. Ray's instincts were to do both, just as he was taught. His deeply held beliefs and training kicked-in at the precise moment and enabled Ray to take action without regard for his life. Accountability trumped all. Complacency was not an option.

After reading Ray's citation for the Distinguished Service Cross, Dr. Matthews felt that Ray's behavior was "occasioned by a firm belief in selfless service, love for fellow soldiers, confidence and competence in his skills, and the psychological and biological effects of mortal stress." In a matter of seconds, he took control of his fears and placed them aside for the good of his soldiers and the unit.

Soldiers who fight in combat or those who face non-combat life threatening situations deal with their fears in different ways. One way, says Dr. Matthews, is to "focus attention on the task at hand and not on personal consequences. A firm sense of the larger meaning of their mission and role is critical, as is the ability to articulate this meaning to themselves and others."

On 18 September 1968, Ray acted in accordance with training received and his deep-rooted personal beliefs. "[Ray's] psychological makeup, his training, and his belief system–when activated–drove him to heroic behavior," said Dr. Matthews. "The same situation might cause some or even many soldiers to freeze or even flee. After all, rewards for heroism are made *because* they are unusual and exemplary." There is one thing I am sure of; neither ego nor arrogance, neither recognition nor glory, were in the forefront of his mind. That was not Ray.

Ray's friends never saw him lead troops in combat. Based on his knowledge of Ray, Glynn surmised, "[Ray] would have been encouraging, but demanding. He would have been hard, but fair. He would have shared his food and ammunition, endured their hardships, and sacrificed for their wellbeing. He was the ideal fighter-leader, and I am sure his men loved him."

The way in which Ray lived his life may not be unique. What was unique, though, was the explosion of selfless acts of courage that took place on the battlefield in Vietnam. His character, education, and training spotlight the reason for the choices he made. His actions provide a glimpse into the heart of this Soldier-leader.

Chapter Fifteen

THE BROTHERHOOD
OF SOLDIERS

"History will show that no man rose to military
greatness, who could not convince his troops
that he put them first."

General Maxwell D. Taylor
USMA 1922

In modern warfare, the U.S. Army has access to the most sophisticated weapons available, but weapon technology alone does not win battles. High tech weapons may be accelerators of warfare but not the basis of winning engagements. Ground Soldiers and tactics win battles, and that takes leaders who can bring Soldiers and units together in the pursuit of a mission. As Battalion Commander, 3rd Battalion, 502nd Infantry, 101st Airborne Division, Harry Rothmann said in his command philosophy, battles "are won by people who know the tools of the trade and who believe in themselves, believe in their fellow soldiers, and believe in their purpose. Effective soldiers win battles through a sense of brotherhood and service, which builds and sustains cohesive combat units."

For centuries, Soldiers who fought in combat saw themselves as part of a unit, a Brotherhood or Band of Brothers. That cohesion exists today. Scene III, *The English Camp,* of Act IV of Shakespeare's play *The Life of King Henry the Fifth,* highlights an insightful reality into the meaning of The Brotherhood of Soldiers. The writings come from an actual event that took place at the Battle of Agincourt in 1415 as the faltering English troops, outnumbered two to one, were about to engage the French cavalry.

From this day to the end of the world,
But we in it shall be remembered-
We few, we happy few, we band of brothers.
For he today that sheds his blood with me
Shall be my brother. Be he ne'er so vile,
This day shall gentle his condition.
And gentlemen in England now abed
Shall think themselves accursed they were not here,
And hold their manhood's cheap whiles any speaks
That fought with us upon Saint Crispin's Day.

The bond formed among Soldiers in combat is a bond not only embraced on the battlefield, but also is often times everlasting, manifested in the unique circumstances they face in hostile environments. It coalesces and strengthens under effective leadership and can be a force that wins battles. Soldiers share hardships. Soldiers share extreme danger. Soldiers share mental anguish. They live under the constant threat of suffering wounds or worse, dying. They share a feeling of "We're all in this together." "There is nothing else like it," said Bill Guinn. "Everyone depends on everyone else. It's like a family."

The bond begins with mutual respect. And, that is a powerful multiplier to unify the unit. Former Commander of the 101st Airborne Division, Major General Burton Patrick, in a speech to his commanders, said,

> You cannot expect a soldier to be a proud soldier if you humiliate him. You cannot expect him to be brave if you abuse and cower him. You cannot expect him to be strong if you break him. You cannot ask for respect and obedience and willingness to face danger if your soldier has not been treated with respect and dignity which fosters unit esprit and personal pride.

> And if you care, if you give a damn, then your soldiers will believe in you and will make the same commitment to service that you must. They will listen, learn, trust, and obey. They will follow and even face death for you.

> And if you [*really*] give a damn, you will focus on them rather than on your superiors, on their performance, and well-being rather than on your advancement and success. You will know them. You

will engender loyalty and you would command a beautifully bonded unit.

Mutual respect comes in many forms. As a leader in combat, Harry Rothmann talked to me about "a passage," when faced with a dangerous situation. Never have your Soldiers do something that you would not do yourself. "It's not easy crawling into a tunnel; I can tell you that much. I had to overcome my fear."

Freed Lowrey believed strongly in respecting his Soldiers. He said, "And, let them know that you respect them. Believe in them, treat them fairly, and take care of them. If you do that, there is not much they won't do for you." He recalled the respect he gave to his men particularly on his second tour. "That's when I fell in love with Soldiers," said Freed. "As long as they knew that you knew your job and you took care of them, they fought like hell. They did it for each other, and they did it for you."

Ray DeVincent said, "You don't want to turn off your own men. [Lt. Enners] never did that. For the short time I was in his platoon, there was no worry. I knew he was there to take care of us."

A fitting example of respect that works both ways occurred on 22 September 1968, after Ray's death, on the hill that occupied Observation Post 7 at the Hà Thanh Special Forces Camp. Hiding in tunnels and fighting from bunkers, an unknown size NVA force engaged Alpha Company, 1-20th Infantry. Shrapnel wounded Lieutenant McNown in the head. As the enemy closed in on his platoon from two sides, a round hit his ammunition magazine and broke the spring. His M16 was inoperable. Sergeant Randy Less covered Lieutenant McNown as he changed his magazine. The NVA fire wounded Sergeant Less, a sucking chest wound–the most serious of its kind. Others in the vicinity were screaming, *Doc, Doc, Sergeant Less is hit.* Doc Bushey rushed to his aid. "He was just lying there, gasping for air," said Doc. Doc pulled Less back behind a rock outfall, covered his wound with plastic, and gave him mouth-to-mouth CPR. He died in a matter of minutes.

Only those that live through the experience of combat truly understand the level of respect and trust that Soldiers have for one another. One can write about these events from research, but the reality and legitimate explanation of The Brotherhood lies with those who comprise The Brotherhood and are a part of the experience.

The bonds of The Brotherhood strengthen with trust. Trust is two-fold. Capability-based trust is the knowledge, both technical and tactical, to lead a unit in combat. It is the ability to solve problems and make decisions based on available information. It can be situational. Character-based trust is developed over time by modeling consistent and predictable behaviors, like open communications, respect for others, integrity, and adherence to other personal values. Both types of trust eventually lead to loyalty in subordinate team members and solidify the bond, often times forever.

A common practice that contributes to this sense of trust and respect in a unit is the After Action Review (AAR). After a mission or combat engagement, the commanding officer or unit leader reviews actions taken during the event with subordinates. Helmets removed, rank discarded for purposes of the discussion, subordinates are encouraged to speak freely. For the officer, he or she gains a valuable, unfiltered critique, and for the NCOs and enlisted personnel, it's a sign of respect whereby they can speak openly about the results of a dangerous combat mission. Harry Rothmann said it was a standing taunt in his platoon. The squad leaders and platoon sergeant assembled after a mission with a beer. Harry would say, "Let's talk about it; how did we do? Why did we run into that ambush? How could we have done better?"

Loyalty is one of the U.S. Army's values. To some, it is one of those elusive terms, difficult to define and a challenge to quantify. However, you know it and feel it when it is present. The Army is clear, *crystal-clear*, on its definition of loyalty: "Bear true faith and allegiance to the U.S. Constitution, the Army, your unit, and other soldiers." As the description suggests, loyalty engenders both vertical and horizontal allegiances, a devotion to the ideals of the unit as a whole (and higher), and devotion to those within the unit. In our discussion, Dr. Matthews indicated that typically "soldiers do not fight for their country or for abstract ideals; rather, they fight for one another." Leaders who train their troops to be competent warriors, respect and treat them fairly, set unifying goals, lead from their values, and display a sense of duty will breed loyalty *and commitment* with the Soldiers in the unit, thereby strengthening The Brotherhood.

Discussing the foundation of The Brotherhood is one thing, but below the surface of the words is what is most important: the actions a leader takes and being accountable for those actions. The best leaders praise their people when the unit performs and take the "heat" (alone) when the unit does not successfully complete the mission. They do not make excuses for shortfalls nor do they lay blame. Leaders set expectations and standards for their people and expect subordinates to "call another out" when a member of the unit is not living up to those standards. If not, it can get Soldiers wounded or killed.

A common display of loyalty is through commitment. Nothing breaks the bond among members of a unit more than the lack of commitment. By virtue of the fact that a Soldier fights in combat, that is a strong commitment. However, commitment goes deeper than that. A solid commitment to support and take care of each other strengthens The Brotherhood. "You become so tight with these people, you're closer than brothers," said Doc Bushey. "You depend on them for your life, and they depend on you." A Soldier wants to know that someone has their "six," has their back.

A Soldier also wants to know that an officer is competent and is looking out for the welfare of the unit as the unit conducts its mission. "Ray always made sure his troops were spread out, whereas some lieutenants were slack and laid back. They let people do what they wanted, let troops bunch up," said Al Matheson. On the afternoon of 18 September, Ray ensured 3rd platoon was spread out. "If we hadn't been, more people would have been hit," said Al. "Ray knew how to soldier; he was well educated and well trained."

Taking care of his Soldiers was a prime requisite of Glynn Hale during his combat tour, but his concept was quite different than one might think. Most believe that if an officer provides Soldiers with a "hot meal and dry socks on the objective and their mail," that is sufficient. After Glynn's first firefight, he had a revelation, an awakening. While those acts of kindness were important, they were mere tokens–his renaissance in thought on the "welfare of soldiers" shifted to what would keep them alive.

Glynn's anecdote of his first horrific firefight against the NVA and VC highlights this realization. He had been a platoon leader for all of five days. His platoon sergeant was only twenty-one years old and squad leaders, nineteen or twenty years of age. Glynn describes:

> The company was conducting a search and destroy mission in the jungle [near Phước Vĩnh in the III Corps Tactical Zone] with platoons operating independent of each other. We came across a well-traveled north-south trail. We moved into a hasty ambush while I reported to the company commander that [it was] my intent to monitor the trail for about thirty minutes and then recon in both directions before continuing my mission. While the first squad

was paralleling the trail to the north, we could faintly hear what sounded like someone occasionally chopping wood to our south. When the first squad returned, I went with the second [squad] to investigate the sound to the south.

We found what turned out to be a company-size base camp occupied by a forty to fifty NVA-VC mixed company (they were called Red Star units when NVA and VC were mixed together). I conducted a leader's recon (a la Ranger school), had another squad join us, and then we open-up on what appeared to be ten to fifteen men sitting around eating, smoking, and joking, and one idiot occasionally chopping on a tree with a machete.

In the brutal firefight that followed, Glynn lost two Soldiers KIA due to an M60 machine gun malfunction–one Soldier literally died in his arms. Six suffered wounds. His unit killed eleven NVA and VC. Glynn was wounded twice, once by a grenade and once by shrapnel from a mortar round tied in a tree designed to simulate a Claymore mine. Glynn continues:

The rest of the company linked up with us that evening. That night, I laid between one of my poncho-wrapped KIAs and my wounded medic. I drifted off to sleep and was awakened by a noise that I realized was the moaning of my medic and me.

That was my first chance to assess and reflect on what had happened that day. It is clear to me even today the words I actually said to myself that night, "This is serious shit." You can intellectualize the effects of combat all you want, but having your face rubbed in it is a sobering, and in some cases, a traumatizing experience.

I had always wanted to be a soldier but discovered that night the price I would have to pay and the commitment I would need to make. That night shaped me for the rest of my career–my soldiers would always be well trained, well led, and I would never have another machinegun malfunction.

"Let no man's ghost say, 'I wish I had been better trained.'"

"If a leader is truly concerned for his soldiers' welfare," said Glynn, "he will ensure they are mentally and physically tough, well trained, and well led." He concluded that, "Soldiers [and] units must be trained under the toughest, most demanding and stressful conditions possible, culminating in realistic live-fire validation." Glynn implemented this philosophy in the 3rd Ranger Battalion and 3rd Brigade, 82nd Airborne Division during his tour in Vietnam with great success.

One of the best expressions of The Brotherhood is the *Esprit d' Corps* that leaders develop in military units. The Manchus, 2nd Battalion, 9th Infantry Regiment, guard the friendly side of the DMZ in South Korea day and night.

In 1925, the Department of War issued a general order permitting this unit *only* to wear a unique belt buckle with their service uniforms. Ed Sullivan served as both S3 (operations) and XO (executive officer) of the 2nd battalion. "When you passed a higher ranking officer and saluted, you would say 'Manchu, Sir' and the officer's reply would be 'Keep up the fire,'" said Ed. At the beginning of the twentieth century during the Boxer Rebellion, that mantra served its purpose for the 9th Infantry Regiment during the Battle of Tientsin, as they were instrumental in quelling riots in Qing, China.

The mantra and belt buckle are only two examples of what the 2nd battalion does to maintain their *Esprit d' Corps*. "When you arrive at the unit, you are given a Manchu plate, a Manchu goblet with a Manchu insignia, a civilian dress belt buckle, and a Manchu drinking suit - a suit with the Manchu insignia on the back." At every officers happy hour, Soldiers are required to wear the suit. When an officer rotates out of his unit, he receives a "mug" with an inscription of choice on it. These types of actions build unit cohesion and The Brotherhood. They are reminders for the Soldiers that comprise the organization of their responsibilities and dedication to the unit, the nation, and its Allies.

The bonding of Alpha Company Soldiers began in 1967 at Schofield Barracks, Hawaii, when the 11th Brigade of the Americal Division was re-activated. Over the course of eight months, they lived together, socialized together, trained in the dense forests of the Kahuku Forest Reserve together and sailed to Vietnam together on the USS *Gordon*. "The camaraderie is what makes you feel good,"

said Al Matheson. "We felt close to one another." To this day members of Alpha Company and 1-20th reunite at annual reunions. Although the ranks are thinning as some have passed on, The Brotherhood of this unit thrives.

What drives unit cohesion long after the sounds of war subside may be a mystery to those who have not experienced the bonds of The Brotherhood in combat. The poem "Why Veterans Reunite," written by a Soldier whose name is unknown, best captures the essence of The Brotherhood.

Why Veterans Reunite
I know why men who have been to war yearn to reunite.
Not to tell stories or look at old pictures. Not to laugh or weep.
Comrades gather because they long to be with men who once acted at their best;
men who suffered and sacrificed, who were stripped of their humanity.

I did not pick these men. They were picked by fate and the military.
But I know them in a way I know no other men.
I have never given anyone such trust.
They were willing to guard something more precious than my life.
They would have carried my reputation, the memory of me.
It was part of the bargain we all made,
the reason we were so willing to die for one another.

As long as I have memory, I will think of them all, every day.
I am sure that when I leave this world,
my last thought will be of my family and my comrades
Ahh, such good men.

Lest we forget those men and women, "such good men [and women]" who place and continue to place their lives on the line for the freedoms we take for granted. It is the least we can do, to honor them and The Brotherhood to which they belong and serve.

A bond also exists among Academy graduates. Four years of education, military training, and athletics cement relationships, not only within each graduating class, but also with all who become a member of the Long Gray Line. This common experience grounded in the values Duty, Honor, Country is at the very least a reason to call these graduates Brothers in Arms–a relationship that can span a lifetime.

Ray's classmate and Class President Thomas B. Dyer III commented on the closeness of the Class of 1967. "It all began in Beast Barracks in the summer of 1963. Plebe Christmas at West Point allowed us all to get to know each other. The next three years of our cadet experience forged our relationships and built what became 'The Brotherhood of '67.' Graduation was the beginning of our lives as Brothers in Arms. Our families and Ray's family were one Family, Brothers in Arms."

Mark R. Hamilton wrote this poignant poem for the Class of 1967's twentieth reunion. Read at the Vietnam Veterans Memorial, it expressed the bond that this class felt. It epitomizes the closeness of the class and its reverence to the fallen.

Reunion
Always we will think of you in sunlight
While hats tossed high in the June air
Turning freely, brass shield and black bill
Shiny as the moment
Held aloft by our collective joy
It seemed that they would not come down
But remain suspended as we turned beneath them
To grasp each other's hands
Up there still, as we sought a certain friend
To say things far too serious for young men
There still, as we hugged the people we had loved
Too long apart
Still there, moving westward
As the impatient planet spun beneath them
It was March when the first one fell,
Soiled and tattered with no hint of sunlight.
Others fell.
We were young men, uncertain how to grieve,
Clinching our jaws against the awful roll call.
The years have changed us all.
Our rings are worn smooth
By the friction of our own flesh.
Young comrades have become companions

With the sharing of our lives,
We have come to share with you again,
As grown men unafraid of sorrow,
And so, unafraid of you
We have gathered for Reunion
To walk together the span of black stone
And see your names blaze white in the sunlight,
See them rise above turning freely,
Held aloft by our collective love,
To join again the white hats
Tossed high in the June air.

If it were not for Ray's Brothers in Arms, the memory of his character, acts of kindness and courage on the battlefield would have died many years ago. From privates to colonels, from letters to eulogies, from tributes to the reading of his name on the Vietnam Veterans Memorial, members of the Class of 1967, the Long Gray Line, and others honored Ray beyond imagination.

As a cadet at West Point, I knew little of what Brothers in Arms did for one another out of respect and honor. After we buried Ray high in the Hudson Highlands, I learned rather quickly.

His Brothers continue to keep his name alive.

Epilogue

A special breed of person serves in our armed forces. When asked, these Soldiers step up, step up proudly.

A special breed of Soldier serves in combat on the front lines and often times places himself or herself in harm's way. It is a call to duty, a chance to show their commitment to this great Nation and its long held beliefs.

Soldiers do not choose the wars they fight, and often times the ideals of anti-war activists and government policy clash. Such was the case during the Vietnam War. Thomas Paine said, "Those who expect to reap the blessings of freedom, must, like men, undergo the fatigues of supporting it." It *is* the price we pay as Americans. It *is* the sacrifice we make, to ensure our way of life.

There is also a special breed of Soldier, who risks their life for one another, for their unit or for the cause of freedom. It is the ultimate act of selfless service. Acts of courage and heroism come in many forms, and in the annals of American history, we have witnessed and heard of them both on and off the battlefield. It is perhaps an obsession with duty or a heightened level of commitment. Character and knowledge fuel these acts. In the final analysis, we must remember–bold deeds save lives. Bold deeds make a difference.

Ray served his country through commitment, courage, and sacrifice, beliefs common among service academy cadets and midshipmen and members of America's Armed Services. His heart of gray embraced all that was West Point.

What saddens me most is what Ray would have accomplished had he lived. We will never know for sure. Whatever the endeavor, I am quite positive he would have served in the military with honor. He would have led based on his character. He would have inspired selflessness. He would have placed the welfare of others before his own. And, he would have spoken through his actions.

I wrote this book, not to invoke sorrow, not to tally the medals or honors bestowed upon him both before and after his death. I wrote *Heart of Gray* so others might learn the value of living one's life with a purpose and make a difference in the life of others.

IN MEMORIAM

"What we have done for ourselves alone dies with us;
what we have done for others, and the world,
remains ... immortal."

Albert Pike

When I began the journey of writing about Ray's life, I thought it sufficient to express my point of view as to who this young man was and the views of classmates and comrades; his personality that touched many, his character that influenced many, and his drive that impressed many.

I would be remiss if I did not include the outpouring of sentiments, the numerous thoughts and comments made by others after his burial at West Point.

What follows are excerpts of tributes from websites and letters from friends, colleagues, acquaintances, and those he served with that were filed away by my mom as remembrances of a son, remembrances of a time long ago. I included only a portion of them.

Maryann E. Ferreri
Supervisor, English Department
Half Hollow Hills High School
30 January 1991

Ray was, is, and always will be a fine example [of a] son, student, young patriot, and hero on the fields of sports and military battle. To say his name–even after these many years since his death in Vietnam, September 18, 1968–is to cause a flood of outstanding memories for each and all of us who were honored to know and love Ray. He was a "once-in-a-lifetime" human being whose footprint will always be found on the sands of time.

★ ★ ★

Ken McEwan
Student
Half Hollow Hills High School
1968

A Man has Fallen

In Vietnam a war rages, out of control to some,
not enough of a conflict to others
It still rages though a man has fallen
Fallen somewhere in a jungle on the other side of the world
To me and many others he was
and will always remain a symbol–that of self-pride

Yes, a man has fallen but to some a legend is born
He is now too distant to reach, too far to climb to
Only in memories will a man named Ray appear in the hearts of many,
not ambiguous, sullen or down-hearted
but clear, majestic and proud

★ ★ ★

Nicholas Messina
President, Student Council
Half Hollow Hills High School Pep Rally
Fall 1969

Six years ago, Ray Enners stood in your place. He shouted and cheered just as you will today. Then he went out on the field and did his best.

Ray graduated this high school and went to West Point. He returned last June to address the Athletic Awards dinner–two months later he was in Vietnam.

First Lieutenant Ray Enners is now gone, but his spirit remains with us. It is this driving, competitive spirit that we are trying to capture today.

We must carry on with this spirit through victory or defeat. And, as Ray Enners did, each of us must go out and do his best.

Edward P. Schreiber
Student
Half Hollow Hills High School

When you are young, there is a tendency to be like someone, someone special; someone like Ray. I was lucky enough to play football and lacrosse with Ray's brother Richie. So our paths crossed, and I am forever grateful. Ray was one we all wanted to be like, the one with great confidence and the one who was always ready to take on challenges. He was always prepared and worked to hone his skills. I remember watching him play [lacrosse] and watching him wait to set up a teammate rather than score himself, the ultimate team player. That and other memories have stayed with me forever.

As a Social Studies teacher for over thirty years, my classes would often discuss issues of leadership and character. I often times reflected on my memories of Ray and how he conducted himself, how hard he worked to achieve his goals in life, how people always looked to Ray for [guidance]. I shared with my classes memories of Ray and told them that I was a better man for having had the opportunity to know [him] and only wished that they would have had the opportunity to know Ray as well. We all need people in life to look up to. Ray was one of mine.

★ ★ ★

James "Ace" F. Adams
Coach of Lacrosse
West Point
22 September 1968

Ray was held in the highest esteem by everyone who knew him, and he will always be remembered with great warmth and affection. His attitude and great effort he put forth were admired by all, as was his always friendly disposition.

Words seem so trite in trying to express my sentiments, but I do want you [Ray's parents] to know that of all the wonderful boys I have come in contact with, none was more sincere or unselfish in regard to his teammates and none better liked and respected by his coaches and fellow players.

★ ★ ★

John Carney
4 September 2002

Iggy Enners–a better man never lived. I remember him with great fondness as a gentle and affirming individual who cared for the little guy. He was a first class athlete, but there was not one wit of pretense or arrogance about him. He was loved by all and died defending America. May he rest in peace.

★ ★ ★

Larry Izzo
Friend, Classmate and Teammate
USMA 1967
11 October 1968

How I wish I could have been at West Point for the funeral. I would have liked to be near Ray once again. But Ray will always be close to me, always.

I want to say that I never met a finer guy. I never knew him to do an unkind act to anyone. I hope someday I'll be lucky enough to have a son like Ray.

★ ★ ★

Chris Pettit
Friend, Classmate and Teammate
USMA 1967
Excerpts from Ray's Memorial

Those who knew Ray at all will never forget him. He exemplified the traits of courtesy, responsibility, and determination at their finest. To his coach, friends, school principal, teachers as well as athletic opponents, his memory is of a man who excelled not only as a scholar and athlete, but also as a human being.

It is through athletic experiences that Ray's nature may be best described. Still vivid over a span of years are the many wonderful memories of Iggy: his quiet joy at victory when his face lit up and he grasped his teammates; his utter disbelief at defeat, as he sat, still in uniform, with tears welling in his eyes; his help and advice to his teammates; the spirit he displayed as a competitor on the field; his love of the game and his respect for all.

There is a void never to be filled, but always bridged by fond, wonderful memories of an outstanding soldier, an uncommon man, and a loving son and friend.

★ ★ ★

Mike Spinello
Friend and Classmate
USMA 1967
18 March 2015

We were young, proud, strong, and ready-and then he was gone. I was on Okinawa when I heard [of his death]. I have mourned and missed him since.

What I have never forgotten was that Iggy visited and encouraged me "cross Corps," and always when our sports were in season, he would actively seek me out and encourage me. I can count my classmates on one hand who were remarkably kind to me and [Iggy] was the first in that group-he never forgot me. I loved him as my friend and brother.

★ ★ ★

Ed Sullivan
Friend, Classmate and Teammate
USMA 1967
27 September 1968

Ray's friendship, his drive, and his determination were an inspiration to me and all of his friends. He never let down, even when he was hurting. And I say without hesitation that Iggy's actions over here [Vietnam] were the same way. He served in the most unselfish way and gave much joy and courage to the people around him.

★ ★ ★

Mike Johns, First Lieutenant
1ˢᵗ Air Calvary Division, Vietnam
17 October 1968

I read the news about Ray in the *Army Times* tonight, and I've never felt more like crying in my life. We live in constant fear over here [Vietnam] and are, therefore, in a bad position to justify this war in our minds.

I consider myself fortunate to have known Ray. There are so few polite and considerate people around anymore. I envied his charismatic qualities. I always will.

Ray and I planned to get together after all this was over. I'll be with Ray someday and then I'll be able to thank him for all he did for me.

★ ★ ★

James H. Keating
Lacrosse Coach
United States Air Force Academy
27 September 1968

During our short but memorable acquaintance, I grew to like and admire Ray very much. We had planned to bring Ray back to the Air Force Academy after his tour in Vietnam. His enthusiasm and outstanding attitude will be greatly missed.

★ ★ ★

Terry L. Woods
Lacrosse player
United States Air Force Academy
23 September 1968

Unselfishly he gave time to teach me and my classmates the finer points of lacrosse last spring. He could have done many other things on those afternoons, but he didn't. He saw some people who needed help, so Lieutenant Enners gave us some assistance.

Lieutenant Enners was gracious in spirit and kind in heart. I have never seen such standards as your son displayed in a world that needs so many more Lieutenant Enners.

Members of the Class of 1969
USMA, Company B-1
21 September 1968

Words cannot begin to express the loss that you must feel. We too feel that loss of a great friend and former Company commander here at B-1.

We all knew Iggy well and respected him for all that he stood for. Company B-1 would be more than proud to serve as the honor guard at his funeral.

Alpha Company
1-20th Infantry, 11th Brigade, Americal Division
26 May 2003

"Greater love hath no man than this; that a man lay down his life for his friends."

Ray Enners was a member of a great rifle company, Alpha Company, 1st Battalion 20th Infantry, 11th Light Infantry Brigade. The men of Alpha Company, his friends, will hold Ray's memory in The Wall of our hearts for all our lives.

Bill Adams, Captain
Commanding Officer, Alpha Company, 1-20th Infantry
7 March 1999

Ray was devoted to his cause and steered his course in his own way. Always mindful of the welfare of his men, he often set an example for others when he withheld his own comforts until his soldiers were cared for. Ray's passing had a significant effect on Alpha. Ironically, my memory peaks the few days before and the few days after Ray was killed.

Rest in peace brother. We will all meet again in the halls of Valhalla along with our comrades.

★ ★ ★

Ray DeVincent
RTO, Alpha Company, 1-20ᵗʰ Infantry
9 October 2014

I liked Ray. He was a decent guy, an absolute decent guy. He would talk to you like you were a human being and like he was a human being. The men loved him as far as I could tell. When ordering the supplies, he was fair to everybody. He understood if supplies were not available. I was happy that the Captain put me in his platoon when I got back from R&R. He was the best lieutenant we had in the company. He was the fairest and the nicest. Guys would fight for him, that's the kind of guy he was.

★ ★ ★

Doug Falck, First Lieutenant
Platoon Leader, Alpha Company, 1-20ᵗʰ Infantry
3 February 1999

I knew you for all too short of time. We shared our platoon, and you affected me more than you ever knew. Rest in peace from Alpha Three-Zero to Alpha Three-Zero.

★ ★ ★

William D. Guinn, Colonel
Commanding Officer, 1-20ᵗʰ Infantry Regiment
2 October 1968

Raymond was an exemplary officer whose absence from our battalion will be keenly felt by all its members. He was an outstanding officer who was liked and respected by all his associates. His compassion for his men and concern for their welfare endeared each and every soldier to him, making his death a shocking experience for all of us.

Al Matheson, Sergeant
Squad Leader, 3rd Squad, 3rd Platoon, Alpha Company, 1-20th Infantry
2 October 2014

I cannot even begin to put a value on my respect for Lt. Raymond Enners, and I will continue to address him as such for the remainder of my life, except in the following sentence. Please tell your mother that I have been blessed with a wonderful wife and son, and a precious granddaughter, and I would not have any of those life fulfillments if it [were] not for the heroism of her son, Ray.

Bill McAlarney, Specialist Fourth Class
RTO 3rd Platoon, Alpha Company, 1-20th Infantry
6 March 2005

Ray, you saved my life making me take the radio in Ha Thanh. I never had a chance to thank you, but if I go to heaven, I know you'll be there. I picture your face often, always with a grin. You are truly missed and never forgotten.

Bill McAlarney
6 October 2015

I knew your brother a very short time, but his face will always be in my heart and he is remembered continuously. I [have ridden] to DC every Memorial Day [for] the last 14 years and pay respects to your brother, a man that made it possible for me to make it back home. He will never be forgotten in my lifetime.

John McNown, Jr., First Lieutenant
Platoon Leader, Alpha Company, 1-20th Infantry
11 November 1999

Ray, I look at your name and I don't know what to say. Even thirty years later, I don't know what to say to you. You were like a ball of fire, all heat and energy. You never did anything halfway. When you drank, you drank deep. When you fought, you fought hard. When your platoon was on point, you often walked slackman. When you smiled, we all smiled. The day you died was the worst day of my life. Guarding your body in the dark waiting for the helicopter to come and take you away was the worst part.

Take care, Ray. I'll see you later on.

★ ★ ★

Kenneth R. Smith, Specialist Fourth Class
Rifleman, 3rd Squad, 3rd Platoon, Alpha Company
2 July 1969

I believe I can honestly say that he was one of the finest people I have had the pleasure knowing. I wrote my parents a numerous amount of letters telling them just what kind of a man he was.

To me he was almost like a father. He was the first human being I ever cried over. Thank you for letting me have the pleasure of knowing such a fine man.

★ ★ ★

Michael A. Voy, Specialist Fourth Class
RTO, 3rd Platoon, Alpha Company
2 July 2004

I was not worthy, but privileged and honored to carry your radio. You will always be remembered as the quintessential warrior.

THOSE WHO FELL
OPERATION CHAMPAIGN GROVE
1ST BATTALION, 20TH INFANTRY

Richard Alan Chambers	PFC17	September 1968	Alpha Company
Willie Charles Hardy	CPL	17 September 1968	Alpha Company
George Lee Jr.	SP4	17 September 1968	Alpha Company
George David Shannon	CPL	17 September 1968	Alpha Company
Raymond James Enners	1LT	18 September 1968	Alpha Company
Gilbert Merill Maestas	SGT	18 September 1968	Alpha Company
Kermit Louis Williams	SGT	18 September 1968	Alpha Company
Gary Lee Browning	SP4	18 September 1968	HHC
Gilford Frank Dashner	CPL	18 September 1968	Delta Company
John Francis Downey Jr.	SSGT	18 September 1968	Delta Company
Charles Lloyd Freeman	SGT	18 September 1968	Delta Company
James Omer Fryman	CPL	18 September 1968	Delta Company
Robert Lawrence Janowitz	1LT	18 September 1968	Delta Company
Alfred M. Schrodeder	1LT	18 September 1968	Delta Company
J.B. Spearmon	SGT	18 September 1968	Delta Company
Donald Eugene Turner	SGT	18 September 1968	Delta Company
James P. Concannon	PFC	21 September 1968	Delta Company
Randall Patrick Less	SGT	22 September 1968	Alpha Company

May They Rest in Peace

Acknowledgments

The inspiration for *Heart of Gray* came in part from the desire to honor my brother and honor West Point, which strongly influenced not only Ray's brief life but also mine as I pursued a career in business after my military obligation. The process was daunting, but at the same time, extremely rewarding. The timing was perfect as it provided the occasion to reflect on all that transpired over the years and place the loss of Ray in perspective.

The writing of this book would not have been possible without the contribution of many. It was truly a team effort. Each brought personal feelings and insightful perspectives on a variety of topics, which complemented Ray's character, courage, and leadership.

I am indebted to members of the Long Gray Line and classmates John S. Caldwell Jr., Thomas B. Dyer, Glynn W. Hale, W. Freed Lowrey, Harry E. Rothmann, Michael T. Spinello, and Edward A. Sullivan, who contributed greatly. Their memories of Ray, thoughts on leadership, importance of The Brotherhood, and anecdotes from their experiences at West Point, in Vietnam, and during their military careers highlight valuable lessons for combat and business leaders. They brought interesting and insightful first-hand accounts in the stories they told.

I am truly grateful to other members of the Long Gray Line. T. Christopher Pettit, teammate, wrote Ray's eulogy and through various tributes kept Ray's name alive. Lawrence L. Izzo, teammate, pledged the lead gift in naming a hallway after Ray at the Kimsey Athletic Center. And William P. Foley, classmate and friend, pledged the lead gift for the Foley·Enners·Nathe Lacrosse Center at Michie Stadium. Warm and heartfelt thanks go to Ray's classmate Lieutenant General John S. Caldwell Jr. (USA Ret.) for writing the Foreword for the book and providing improvements to its content. To Ray's classmates, I am eternally grateful.

I would like to thank Steven F. Wood (USMA 1971), my classmate and team-mate, for contact information on selected interviewees and our many friends who provided their encouragement to pursue this project.

Two other individuals also contributed valuable stories based on their memories of Ray. Mary Anne Pettit clarified the origins of Ray's nickname Iggy and provided fond memories of her time at West Point with Chris Pettit and Ray. Edward P. Schreiber, my high school teammate and classmate, spoke to his students of Ray's character, courage, and leadership as he taught his students high school Social Studies.

The Vietnam Veterans from Alpha Company and the 1-20th, who served with Ray, provided the realism of war and insights into close-order combat that became the basis for a large portion of the book. Reliving and talking about their experiences, I am sure, was agonizing, and I am grateful for their courage to do so and their support in this project. The extensive interviews conducted in person and on the phone and follow-up discussions provided invaluable recollections of Ray and combat events that added emotion and realism to the book. Their memory of events was incredible. I am deeply indebted to David "Doc" Bushey for his graphic recollections as Senior Medic in Alpha Company. Raymond J. DeVincent and William McAlarney provided striking stories and anecdotes of what it was like to be an enlisted Soldier on the front line in combat. From a battalion commander's perspective, William D. Guinn offered his insight into Operation Champaign Grove, the NVA, and VC. Alfred H. Matheson's perceptive view of events he experienced in Vietnam, particularly 17 and 18 September 1968, as well as the challenges of being a squad leader in an infantry rifle platoon provided imagery and realism. John R. McNown furnished aerial images and photographs of the battlefields and brought to light details of the firefights at Câo Nguyên, Xã Ky Mao and Hà Thanh. And a thank you to Sario Caravalho for his support in the project. Kitty Millard and Walter Veto were helpful in providing contact information for some of those who participated.

I would like to thank Thomas R. Cafaro (USMA 1971), teammate and class-mate, for his thoughts on receiving the First LT. Raymond J. Enners Award in 1971 and Douglas Schreiber for his high school memories of Ray and thoughts on winning the same award in 1973. By wearing Ray's jersey number 26 in their professional and collegiate lacrosse pursuits, Doug's son and daughter keep Ray's name alive. Many thanks to Kieran Mullins, winner of the Suffolk County LT. Raymond Enners Award, for his thoughts on what the award meant to him as well as Islip High School Lacrosse Coach Keith Scheidel's comments on the importance of the award.

I would like to thank Jim "Ace" F. Adams, a topflight athlete at Johns Hopkins University, Head Coach of Lacrosse at West Point, the University of Pennsylvania, and the University of Virginia. As one of Ray's mentors, Jim's memories of Ray playing lacrosse at the Academy underscored his fondness for Ray. Our family appreciated his undying support and heartfelt personal comments.

Several authors provided inspiration and valuable guidance on content and structure of the book for which I am grateful. Richard Barlow Adams (USMA 1967), *The Parting: A Story of West Point on the Eve of the Civil War;* Joyce K. Faulkner, *Windshift;* Mark Lee Greenblatt, *Valor: Unsung Heroes from Iraq, Afghanistan and the Home Front;* and Kevin Maurer, *No Easy Day: The Firsthand Account of the Mission that Killed Osama Bin Laden.* All were instrumental in providing alternate points of view that challenged my thinking.

Ronald Wolford Blair, author of *Wild Wolf: The Great Civil War Rivalry* and Jennifer A. Holik, *The Tiger's Widow: A Woman Who Took up the Fight, the Story of Virginia Brouk* were instrumental in advising contacts for publishers and archived military documents. Dr. Michael D. Matthews, Professor of Engineering Psychology at West Point, provided valuable insight into why Soldiers perform heroic acts at the risk of their own lives. To them I am grateful.

I am eternally grateful to the associates at Acclaim Press; Douglas Sikes for his counsel, Editor Randy Baumgardner for his professional advice and ideas, Jeanne Wilson for her countless hours of proofing that immeasurably improved the manuscript and Monica Burnett for her tireless efforts in helping to market the book.

Lieutenant Colonel JD Lock (USA Ret.), *The Coveted Black and Gold: A Daily Journey Through the U.S. Army Ranger School Experience*, and Colonel Ralph "The Ranger" Puckett (USA Ret.) placed me in touch with individuals from the U.S. Army's Airborne and Ranger Training Brigade, who provided entrance and graduation data for Ranger School, Class 4. Without the assistance of Command Sergeant Major Curtis H. Arnold, Sergeant First Class Danny J. Shedd, and Sergeant First Class Gerald L. Nelson Jr., these statistics would not have been included.

Without the assistance of those at West Point who researched my formidable personal requests, the book would have been without factual data. I would like to thank all those who contributed. Joe Alberici, lacrosse coach at West Point, and Matthew A. Falkner provided lacrosse statistics during the years Ray played. Marie C. Lewis (USMA 2004), Associate Director, Class and Membership Services; and Lieutenant Colonel Ron Whittle, Chief Accessions Division, provided statistics on branch selection for the Class of 1967. Lieutenant Colonel Holly F.

West, PhD, Associate Dean for Strategy, Policy and Assessment; and Olga Makhova, Assistant Director Data Services, provided data on entrance and graduation statistics. Suzanne Christoff, Associate Director for Unique Resources, and Elaine McConnell, Rare Book Curator at Jefferson Hall, dug deep to provide The Honorable Stanley R. Resor's graduation speech. Elizabeth A. Barrett and Todd A. Browne (USMA 1985 Colonel USA Ret.) at the Association of Graduates provided a picture of the Foley·Enners·Nathe Lacrosse Center.

A hearty thanks to Rebecca L. Collier, Assistant Chief, Textual Reference Archives; and Jason Staton Sr., Archives Technician at the National Archives in College Park, Maryland, for providing After Action Reports, press clippings, and Daily Journals of combat activities in Vietnam. Norman Richards, Assistant Historian 90th Division Association, at AAA Military Research provided morning reports and Jaclyn Lee, Archives Technician at the National Personnel Records Center, provided personnel records. I thank you.

Dad and Mom did not live to see the release of this book. I think they would have been proud. A pack rat of sorts, Mom kept all of Ray's letters from West Point, Ranger School, Fort Carson, and Vietnam. She kept a detailed scrapbook from high school filled with photographs and news clippings of Ray's earlier years and scrapbook from West Point filled with the same. She also kept pieces of memorabilia and the "black book" he carried into battle filled with mission briefings and a listing of Soldiers under his command. I have vivid memories of the stories they told as Ray was growing up and Dad's stories about his own military service in North Africa. All proved invaluable as they brought Ray's personality and accomplishments to life in various segments of the book. To them I am forever grateful–not only for their sharing of memories, but for their love and support throughout my life.

Finally, yet most importantly, I am eternally grateful to my wife Judy, sons Sean and Ryan, and their families for their encouragement and support during the writing of the book. Judy read and reread the manuscript, helping to make it better. She enthusiastically supported the many hours spent at the local library. A special note of thanks to my sister Sandra Brown, who was an important contributor and source of encouragement along the way. She is the best sister a brother could have.

With a great deal of gratitude and admiration, I wish to applaud all those who served in Vietnam. Over 58,200 did not return home alive, and many of those who did continue to live with the scars of war.

Sources

Books

Ambrose, Stephen E. *Duty, Honor, Country: A History of West Point*. Baltimore: The Johns Hopkins University Press, 1966.

Ambrose, Stephen E. *The Victors: Eisenhower and his Boys: The Men of World War II*. New York: Simon & Schuster, 1998.

Anderson, David L., Chatfield, Charles, edited by John Whiteclay Chambers II. *The Oxford Companion to American Military History*. New York: Oxford University Press, 1999.

Atkinson, Rick. *The Long Gray Line: The American Journey of West Point's Class of 1966*. New York: Picador, 1989.

Chambers, John Whiteclay II. *The Oxford Companion To American Military History*. New York: Oxford University Press, 1999.

Charlton, James. *The Military Quotation Book*. New York: St. Martin's Press, 2002.

Clavell, James. *Sun Tzu: The Art of War*. New York: Bantam Doubleday Dell, 1983.

Clearly, Thomas. *The Art of War: Complete Text and Commentaries*. Boston: Shambhala Publications, Inc., 2003.

Duffy, Neil. *The Spirit in the Stick*. Duffy Publishing, 2010. *Fly to Honor*. Duffy Publishing, 2014.

Fehrenbacher, Don E. *Lincoln: Speeches and Writings 1859-1865, Speeches, Letters, Misc. Writings, Presidential Messages and Proclamations*. New York: Literary Classics of the U.S., 1989.

Gostick, Adrian and Chester Elton. *All In: How the Best Managers Create a Culture of Belief and Drive Big Results*. New York: Free Press, 2012.

Griffin, Darrell. *Business With a Purpose: Starting, Building, Managing and Protecting Your New Business*. Denver: Outskirts Press, 2010.

Hennessey, Patrick. *The Junior Officers' Reading Club: Killing Time & Fighting Wars*. London: Penguin Group, 2009.

Hesselbein, Frances and General Eric K. Shinseki (USA Ret.). *Be · Know · Do*: *Leadership The Army Way*. San Francisco: Jossey-Bass, 2004.

Hoang, Ngoc Lung. *The General Offensive of 1968-69*. U.S. Army Center of Military History, 1981.

Jennings, Eric T. *Imperial Heights: Dalat and the Making and Undoing of French Indochina, From Indochina to Vietnam: Revolution and War in a Global Perspective*. Oakland: University of California Press, 2011.

Kaiser, David E. *American Tragedy: Kennedy, Johnson, and the Origins of the Vietnam War*. Cambridge: Harvard University Press, 2000.

Lock, JD. *The Coveted Black and Gold: A Daily Journey Through the U.S. Army Ranger School Experience*. Bloomington: Xlibris Corporation, 1993.

Masland and Radway, *Soldiers and Scholars*, provided by Stephen E. Ambrose in *Duty, Honor, Country: A History of West Point*. Baltimore: The Johns Hopkins University Press, 1966.

Mastroianni, George R., Susann Kimmelman, Joe Doty, and Joseph J. Thomas. *Leadership in Dangerous Situations*. Edited by Patrick J. Sweeney, Michael D. Matthews, and Paul B. Lester. Annapolis: Naval Institute Press, 2011.

Nahas, Albert J. *Warriors Remembered*. Indianapolis: IBJ, 2010.

Nolan, Keith William. *The Magnificent Bastards: The Joint Army-Marine Defense of Dong Ha, 1968*. New York: Presidio Press, 1994.

Palmer, Dave Richard. *Summons of the Trumpet: U.S.-Vietnam in Perspective*. Novato, California: Presidio Press, 1978.

Rice, Daniel E. and Lieutenant Colonel John A. Vigna (USA Ret.). *West Point Leadership: Profiles of Courage*. Leadership Development Foundation, 2013.

Scruggs, Jan C. and Joel L. Swerdlow. *To Heal a Nation*. New York: Harper & Row, 1985.

Shakespeare, William. *Shakespeare: The Complete Works*. Edited by G.B. Harrison. New York: Harcourt, Brace & World, 1948.

Spector, Ronald H. *After Tet: The Bloodiest Year in Vietnam*. New York: The Free Press, 1993.

Summers, Harry G., Jr. *On Strategy: A Critical Analysis of the Vietnam War*. New York: Random House, 1982.

Taylor, Maxwell D. *West Point Looks Ahead*. New York: West Point, 1946.

USCC. *Bugle Notes*. Newark: Colyer-Roux, 1963.

Wells, Thomas. *The Oxford Companion to American Military History*. Edited by John Whiteclay Chambers II. New York: Oxford University Press, 1999.

Weyand, Alexander M. and Milton R. Roberts. *The Lacrosse Story*. Baltimore: Garamond/Pridemark Press, 1965.

Periodicals

Assembly. Publication of the West Point Alumni Foundation, Inc., Vol. XXX, No. 3, 1971.

Tenth Anniversary Vietnam Veterans Memorial (Official Program Guide). Publication of the Vietnam Veterans Memorial Fund, November 1992.

Pooper Scooper. Publication of West Point, April 2012, September 2012 and April/May 2013 editions.

New York Times. June 8, 1945.

Trident. Publication of the 11th Infantry Brigade, Americal Division, 23 August 1968.

West Point. Publication of the West Point Association of Graduates, winter 2013, Volume 5, Issue 4, fall 2015, Volume 5, Issue 1, winter 2015, and Volume 6, Issue 1, winter 2016.

Documents

A Brief History of the Academy. West Point History. West Point. 2014.

Academy Leadership, LLC. *Leadership Excellence Course.* 2014

All-American History 1967. United States Intercollegiate Lacrosse Association.

Allied Troop Levels 1960-1973. American War Library. 1988.

Association of Graduates, West Point, New York.

Barringer, Mark and Thomas Wells. *The Anti-War Movement in the United States.* Modern American Poetry.

Blobaum, Dean. *Protests at Democratic National Convention in Chicago.* History. August 2008.

Cannon, Chuck and Toby Keith. *American Soldier.* Sung by Toby Keith. Wacissa River Music, 2003.

Card, Michael J. *Draft Morning.* Sung by The Byrds. Mole End Music, 1968.

Collins, Jim. *Leadership Lessons from West Point.* Jim Collins. August 31, 2011.

Combat Action Report Champaign Grove, 1st Battalion, 20th Infantry. 29 September 1968.

Combat Operations After Action Report, 11th Infantry Brigade, Americal Division. National Archives and Records Administration, U.S. Government.

Counteroffensive, Phase V, I July 1968–1 November 1968. U.S. Army.

Cyrus, Billy Ray. *Some Gave All.* Mercury Records, 1992.

DD Form 53-55 WD AGO, Enlisted Record and Report of Separation. p. 63. 15 April 1946 and Form 100 WD AGO, Separation Qualification Record.

Department of the Army, Headquarters, United States Army Vietnam, General Orders Number 403. 5 February 1969.

First Squadron, First Cavalry, First Regiment of Dragoons-Hill 29, 1968. Vietnam War Journal. Hill 29 September.

General Order 582, Article I. President of the Republic of Vietnam. 20 December 1968.

Gibson, Robert D. *Virtue Under Fire: Leadership Attributes Required in the 21ˢᵗ Century Combat*. Indiana University of Pennsylvania. 7 August 2008.

Gill, Kathy. *The Whole World is Watching–August 1968*. About. 28 August 1968.

Harms, Roger D., Richard K. Lipsett, William P. Honjiyo, Conn J. Orville, and Blair Larson. *The History of the 1ˢᵗ Battalion 20ᵗʰ Infantry History in Vietnam*. 1-20 Infantry. 1 February 2006.

Hà Thanh Under Attack. Gia Vuc. Gia Vuc Tribute. August 1968.

Kennedy, John F. (President). *Graduation Address, Class of 1962 United Sates Military Academy, West Point*. "Administration of National Security, selected Papers." District of Columbia: U.S. Government Printing Office, 1962.

Kindig, Jessie. *Student Activism at UW: Vietnam War: Student Activism, 1948-1970*. University of Washington. 2008.

Larned, Charles W. *History of Battle Monument at West Point*. Open Library. West Point, New York. 1898.

Legends and Traditions of the Corps, West Point Parents Club of Washington. 2011.

Living the Army Values. Go Army. U.S. Army.

Long Island Metropolitan Lacrosse Foundation and LIMLF Hall of Fame.

MacArthur, General Douglas. *Duty, Honor, Country*. American Rhetoric, Top 100 Speeches. West Point AOG. West Point. 12 May 1962.

McChrystal, General Stanley (USA Ret.). *Leadership is a Choice*. You Tube. Speech given to students at the Stanford Graduate School of Business. 17 February 2012.

McDonald, Robert. *Values Based Leadership*. Proctor & Gamble. Speech given to several U.S. Universities. 2008 and 2009.

McKinney, Michael. *Generosity*. Leadership Now. M2 Communications.

National Security Action Memorandum No. 273. The White House Washington, lbjlib.utexas.edu/johnson/archives.hom

Paine, Thomas. *The American Crisis: Philadelphia, Sept. 12, 1777*. U.S. History. Independence Hall Association.

Patton, George S. *General George S. Patton, Jr. Quotations*. Estate of General George S. Patton Jr.

Peters, Gerhard and Woolley, John T. *Ronald Reagan: Remarks at the United States Military Academy in West Point, New York*. The American Presidency Project.

Powers, Rod. *The United States Military Academy.* west-point.org

Resor, Stanley R., Secretary of the Army. *Graduation Address, Class of 1967, United States Military Academy, West Point.* Jefferson Hall: West Point. 7 June 1967.

Seketa, Charles S. *Daily Recap of Operations.* 1ˢᵗ Battalion, 20ᵗʰ Infantry. 1 February 2006.

Statistical Information on Casualties of the Vietnam War. National Archives and Records Administration, United States Government. 2010.

Suffolk County Sports Hall of Fame.

Sullivan, General Gordon R. (USA Ret.). *Upon receiving the Sylvanus Thayer Award.* West Point AOG. 1 October 2003.

Taylor, Maxwell D., Gov Leaders.

The State Historical Society of Missouri. Ex-POWs Oral History Project, Stanley A. Tyron. Columbia, Missouri, 2000. 19 January 2001.

Trà, Trần Văn. *Vietnam: History of the Bulwark B2 Theatre, Vol. 5: Concluding the 30-Years War.* Ho Chi Minh City, 1982.

U.S. Army Airborne and Ranger Training Brigade, Fort Benning, Georgia.

U.S. Department of State, Office of the Historian, Document 201, Vol. 1, Vietnam, 1964, 5 June 1964 Foreign Relations of the United States, 1964-1968. District of Columbia: U.S. Government Printing Office.

U.S. Marines in Vietnam: The Defining Years. Marines.

Vietnam. The History Place, Vietnam War.

United States Military Academy Library Archives. West Point, New York.

Vietnam War: The Jungle War 1965-1968. The History Place.

Wall of Faces. Vietnam Veterans Memorial Fund.

Washington, George. *Sentiments on a Peace establishment,* 2 May 1783 writings 26:374-76, 388 91 from Article 1, Section 8, Clause 12, Document 6. The Founders' Constitution, The University of Chicago Press and The Liberty Fund.

About the Author

Author Richard Enners grew up in Farmingdale, Long Island, New York, graduated from the United States Military Academy at West Point in 1971, and served five years in the Army with the 9th Division in Fort Lewis, Washington and the United States Military Academy Preparatory School in Fort Belvoir, Virginia. He later pursued a career in business, initially sales and marketing, and eventually led companies with revenues of $60M-$120M in Japan, British Columbia, and the USA.

Enners wrote *Heart of Gray* not to invoke sorrow, not to tally his brothers awards and accolades-but to honor his brother and to inspire others to live their lives with a purpose just as Ray did and to make a difference in the lives of others.

Richard has two sons Sean and Ryan, Sean living in Golden, Colorado and Ryan in Bedford, New Hampshire. Richard and his wife currently reside in Lexington, Kentucky.

INDEX